FIT

IMPROVING THE LEADERSHIP HEALTH
OF YOURSELF AND OTHERS

Jay R. Desko, Ph.D.   David A. Marks, D.Min.

ACKNOWLEDGMENTS

The Center is a non-profit Christian consulting group whose highly trained team is passionate about advancing leadership and organizational health. We believe this book on being an effective team leader will be a helpful resource for you and your organization. We are providing this resource as an extension of our vision of advancing organizational health.

While The Center and the authors have used their best efforts in producing this book, they make no representations with respect to the accuracy or completeness of its contents. The advice provided may not be appropriate for your specific situation. You should seek professional counsel where appropriate.

For more information about The Center, call us at 215-723-2325 or visit our website www.centerconsulting.org. The Center offices are located at 820 Route 113, Souderton, PA 18964.

All characters appearing in this work are fictitious. Any resemblance to real persons, living or dead, is purely coincidental.

THE CENTER
Guiding Organizations. Coaching Leaders.

TABLE OF CONTENTS

Don't judge each day by the harvest you reap but by the seeds that you plant.

Robert Louis Stevenson

CHAPTER ONE

LEAD WELL

BY JAY R. DESKO, Ph.D.

Like physical fitness, becoming a fit leader does not happen by accident. It requires constant learning, monitoring, and practice. But once you become a reasonably healthy and effective leader, it is easy to slide into bad habits and unhealthy patterns. Before you know it, you're back down to lifting five pounds when your team members need you to be lifting 50! This book will help you get your leadership back into shape by focusing on your health and also your team's health.

DO IT WELL

If you are going to lead, lead well! – Apostle Paul

Do you ever remember hearing your mom or dad say, "If you are going to do something, do it right!"? That advice resonates with what the Apostle Paul said in the Bible. If you are gifted to do something, do it well. Not half-hearted. Not halfway. In other words, lead well.

THOSE WHO LEAD WELL ARE GIFTED YET BROKEN

What do a corporate CEO, pastor, social worker, police officer, and medical doctor all have in common? Certainly not their salary! Each has the responsibility to have a positive impact in the lives of others and the community. But, they have one more thing in common – each has a broken internal GPS that left unchecked will lead to self-centered choices and sometimes even harmful actions against themselves and others. Each of them has the opportunity to influence others for good… or for bad.

While we all are gifted to be difference-makers, each of us is a bit broken as well. We often believe we know better than the one who created us. Such arrogance and independence can result in us impacting others in damaging ways. This is true whether we are pastors, church members, business owners, or employees. Left on our own, we are lost and don't know it, and we are taking others with us!

From the beginning of human civilization, when God first created people, they have acted like they know better than Him and subsequently ignore his instructions. People have continued to try to be like God and expect others to be like Him as well. We expect others to know it all, do it all, and be everywhere we need them to be… all at the same time! For example, organizations and their stakeholders often want leaders who are: strong yet sensitive; decisive yet collaborative; confident yet humble; and visionary yet flexible.

Idolatry begins with the counterfeiting of God, because only with a counterfeit of God can people remain the center of their lives and loyalties, autonomous architects of their futures. Something within creation will then be idolatrously inflated

to fill the God-shaped hole in the individual's world. But a
counterfeit is a lie, not the real thing. It must present itself
through self-deception, often with images suggesting that the
idol will fulfill promises for the good life.
– Richard Keyes, *No God But God*

Just as our predecessors, we are often quick to accept the
challenge and then work hard to fulfill such unrealistic
expectations. All the while, we are striving to be something
or someone we are not. We really like the perks of being
perceived as super-humans. Just as people have made
sacrifices to their gods throughout history, leaders today also
like the VIP treatment. They receive this when they are able to
temporarily act with success in being like god to those around
them! Author Bob Goff calls this identity theft – stealing God's
identity and abusing it! Research has shown such leaders can
easily begin to develop a propensity toward pride, isolation,
and entitlement. Leaders who are elevated to almost divine-
like statuses are provided the perks of deity and expected
to act like gods. They will sometimes begin to believe their
own press, often causing harm to themselves and others. The
ultimate results most commonly consist of anxiety, burnout,
disappointment, and disillusionment.

Narcissistic personalities… are frequently encountered in top
management positions. Indeed, it is only to be expected that
many narcissistic people, with their need for power, prestige,
and glamour, eventually end up in leadership positions. Their
sense of drama, their ability to manipulate others, their knack
for establishing quick, superficial relationships serve them
well in organizational life.
– Manfred F. R. Kets De Vries, *Leaders, Fools, and Impostors*

However, God's reminder from thousands of years ago is a timely one for today's leaders as well: "This is what the LORD says – I am the first and I am the last; apart from me there is no God" (Isaiah 44:7), and "Do not put your trust in princes, in mortal men, who cannot save. When their spirit departs, they return to the ground; on that very day their plans come to nothing" (Psalm 146:3-4).

THOSE WHO LEAD WELL USE INFLUENCE OVER COERCION

What is influence? It is action that results in causing change in someone without using force or coercion. An influential leader is someone who has a positive impact on the people and the organization which he or she serves and does so consistently over a long period of time. These leaders are not super-human but they are different. What makes them influential leaders is first *who* they are and second *what* they do.

We all can be leaders that have a positive influence, regardless of our position. Why? Because positive influence does not require a position, only a relationship. God creates each of us with intrinsic worth and with the ability to influence or lead, some on a large scale and others on a small scale. Some are charismatic communicators, others are strategic thinkers. Some are quiet influencers, others are big and bold.

THE POWER TO INFLUENCE

Power is the capacity to impact the behaviors or thoughts of others and is essential to carry out the legitimate responsibilities found within formal leadership roles. There are three main types of power:

Positional	Expert	Relational
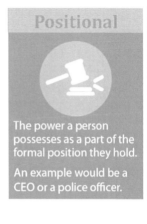		
The power a person possesses as a part of the formal position they hold.	The power a person possesses due to special knowledge or experience.	The power a person possesses because of the personal credibility and trust that has been earned over time.
An example would be a CEO or a police officer.	An example would be a surgeon or a lawyer.	

While it is appropriate and, at times, essential that leaders utilize their positional power and expert power, it is healthier for the leaders, followers, and the overall organization when leaders develop and first depend upon their relational power (often referred to as "relational capital"). While not everyone has an official leadership position or unique expertise, everyone can acquire relational power. In other words, every person has an opportunity to lead regardless of position or title.

> **"**
> Nearly all men can stand adversity, but if you want to test a man's character, give him power.
> – Abraham Lincoln

Due to our desire for control, when a person does not possess positional, expert, or relational power or feels his or her power is not working, he often resorts to coercion – the use of threat or intimidation to get a person or group to do what he wants. While there are unique circumstances where coercion is warranted, it should be the exception rather than the norm. This is because coercion can have long-term and unintended consequences and result in others going silent or withdrawing from the relationship or organization.

FOLLOWER FIRST, LEADER SECOND

A wise leader is first a good follower. Why? Because we need the kind of help that can only be provided by one who is so much greater than ourselves. Seldom will you hear a leader talk about submission. In the minds of many, it is the opposite of leadership and a sign of weakness. Yet, when we submit ourselves to God, He changes us, teaches us, shapes us, and guides us.

Remember, Jesus is not just a role model for a leader. He is the source of our forgiveness, renewal, significance, and hope. When he is placed first and we submit our desires and will to him, we will lead differently. Not perfectly, but differently. Over time, our motives will increasingly become his motives and our self-centeredness will increasingly become other-centeredness. Our lust for more power, possessions, and prestige will increasingly become a desire for having a positive influence on others. Not all at once, and not perfectly, but we will definitely be different.

In his book *The Power of Followership*, management professor Robert Kelly estimates 70%-90% of a typical day is spent in follower type roles.

TALENT + DISCIPLINE = EFFECTIVENESS

One of the things that makes a proverb really interesting is if it rings true to life experience. This is true of Proverbs 14:23: "All hard work brings a profit, but mere talk leads only to poverty." Talent is important, but talent plus discipline is what differentiates a good leader from a great one. Psychologists refer to this discipline as "grit." Other words that infer this trait are focus, hard work, and determination. Some people talk about wanting to start a business; others do it. Some talk about wanting to finish college; others do it. Some people talk about saving money; others do it. You get the point. In addition to talent, effectiveness requires work, and a lot of it.

The most common trait I have seen in people who have started successful businesses, in pastors who are leading growing churches, or in CEOs who are directing effective non-profits is hard work over a long period of time. I do appreciate the growing emphasis today on "life balance" and "quality of life." After all, we all know leaders whose personal drive led to the destruction of their marriages, families, and even resulted in addiction. But sometimes, I often wonder if leaders are forgetting that discipline and hard work are not the enemy to life balance, but rather a vital part of it. We have been deeply shaped by the industrial revolution and the concept of counting work hours. However, throughout much of history, such counting would not have been considered. In an agrarian society, farmers did not count hours; they counted how much food they were going to need to provide for their families! They were far more goal oriented than hour oriented.

Some leaders are working toxic hours and experiencing the side effects in their health and relationships. However, there are other leaders who are not overworking but are over extending themselves in other areas of their lives, believing their job is the source of their stress! This includes the demands of children's activities (what author Kevin DeYoung called kindergarchy – rule by children!) and personal recreation. Both are good, but both can drain our time bank and even our finances and result in a different kind of stress. Remember, being an influential leader requires more than academic credentials, talk, or charm. It requires hard work. Don't fear it; embrace it!

FINISHING WELL

Have you ever watched a person, team, or organization have a strong start and poor finish?

- A teacher who is exciting the first few days and then a dud.
- A soccer game when the team scores the first three goals, only to lose.
- A new business that breaks all expectations, but then sinks.
- A staff member who loves the organization they serve, but leaves with a bad attitude.
- A couple that did a lot of things right as newlyweds, yet divorced 20 years later.
- A movie that captures you for the first ten minutes, but leaves you with regret by the end.
- A well respected leader who inspired you for years, but drifted into a moral mess.

Get the point? Finishing well should be one of the greatest values and goals for any leader. I remember coaching a client who told me, "I did not handle leaving very well at my past position. I want to leave better this time." That is a sign of maturity and growth. Progress, not perfection. This is what every leader should aspire to do and what every Christian leader must aspire to do. From my experience, there are a few distinctives that differentiate those who finish well from those who do not. Those who finish well . . .

1. Embrace a commitment to and a passion for finishing well.
2. Are not perfect and do not let a mistake or failure permanently define them.

3. Surround themselves with others who model living well, leading well, and finishing well.

I alone cannot change the world, but I can cast a stone across the water to create many ripples. – Mother Teresa

The chapters in this book are written from experience. They are themes of importance that we have learned from years of guiding organizations and coaching leaders. These are themes we are continuing to learn ourselves since on this earth we can only experience progress, not perfection. In particular, this book will focus on what contributes to leaders growing in their health and effectiveness…or in other words, becoming FIT! ■

EXERCISE

Do I know my primary areas of brokenness? Am I managing them appropriately?

How do I manage failure in myself and in those around me?

How well am I doing at following and submitting in my life?

Am I utilizing relational influence more than positional power?

To what extent am I manifesting hard work and self-discipline in my life and leadership?

Am I surrounding myself with others who model living well, leading well, and finishing well?

WHAT WE ACHIEVE

—— INWARDLY ——

WILL CHANGE OUR
OUTER REALITY

PLUTARCH

CHAPTER TWO

CULTIVATING TRUST IN YOUR ORGANIZATION

BY JAY R. DESKO, Ph.D.

TRUST DEFINED

Few would question that the Christian life is built upon trust. The primary focus of over 150 references in the Bible related to the theme of trust can be summarized by the following phrase:

> Be quick to trust in God and be slow to trust in people.

We need to consider two aspects of this summary. First, the Bible regularly instructs us to place our trust in God since He is always reliable and His truths are worthy of our confidence. God always fulfills His own expectations. However, He does not always meet our expectations of Him, sometimes resulting in our resistance to further trust Him and His Word.

Second, it is important to avoid substituting the word never for the word slow. Why is it that we should be so cautious to trust in others? A sound biblical anthropology clearly highlights that people are corrupt by nature and not consistently trustworthy (Genesis 3, Jeremiah 17:9). However, in spite of this truth, churches, businesses, governments, families, and society could not function or survive without a basic level of trust. Christian leaders play a strategic role in cultivating a culture where trust is corporately valued and intentionally pursued at home, church, and work.

> Trust is the reliance or confidence that a person or group will meet our expectations of them.

In today's organizations, a variety of buzz words and themes are circulating such as: teamwork, vision casting, mentoring, change management, and empowerment. Each of these roles and related tasks are dependent upon trust. With a low trust culture, it is difficult or impossible to successfully accomplish any one of these, since each is heavily dependent upon trust and trustworthiness.

BASIC ASSUMPTIONS RELATED TO TRUST

Trust always begins with an element of faith and risk. The faith is that a person or organization will meet our expectations; the risk is that they will not. When people fail to meet our expectations, trust is broken and disappointment results, making it more difficult to trust in the future. As a result, trust is hard to acquire and very easy to lose. In addition, once trust is lost, it cannot be regained without once again manifesting trust. In other words, it takes trust to build trust. As a result, trust is fragile and never permanent, requiring constant attention and monitoring.

HOW TRUST WORKS

The 6 Trust Gauges graphically describe how trust works among people and in organizations. All people have expectations of themselves and others. The expectations that are held may not be understood, agreed upon, or fair. These expectations fall into one or more of the following categories: communication, character, concern, competence, connectedness, and consistency. Trust is built when we prove reliable by meeting the expectations others have of us in these six areas.

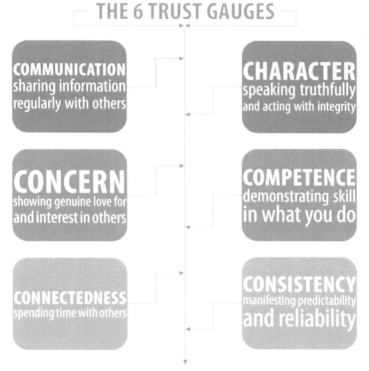

THE 6 TRUST GAUGES

COMMUNICATION sharing information regularly with others

CHARACTER speaking truthfully and acting with integrity

CONCERN showing genuine love for and interest in others

COMPETENCE demonstrating skill in what you do

CONNECTEDNESS spending time with others

CONSISTENCY manifesting predictability and reliability

EXPECTATIONS

People often have differing expectations and do not know it because they have never honestly discussed and agreed upon the expectations. The more we successfully meet the expectations others have of us, the more they will perceive us through the filter of "this is a trustworthy person." Distrust develops when we fail to live up to the expectations others have of us in one or more of the six areas. This distrust then becomes a filter through which most of our other actions or behaviors are judged.

Often, it is assumed that since a person, group, or organization claims to be following Christ, they are trustworthy. As a result, it is further assumed they will act in our best interest, do the right thing, and desire to honor God. However, there are numerous examples of the danger and destruction associated with presumed innocence, including people being sold products or given financial advice that ultimately resulted in loss for them and gain for others. Presumption of innocence must be balanced with accountability and due diligence in investigating the trust record of another person or group.

Christians sometimes operate with a presumption of innocence when dealing with others who profess faith in Christ.

One of the ways we practice due diligence is by seeking the endorsement of others regarding someone's trustworthiness. If someone we trust endorses the trustworthiness of someone else, we are more inclined to trust that person as well. On the other hand, if someone we trust believes another person should not be trusted, we are less likely to trust that person. This initial perception formation is one way trust is initially acquired or lost.

PERCEPTION

Perceptions are cognitive pictures that are stored in the brain. They develop as a result of a complex combination of factors including concrete experiences, cultural beliefs, and social influences. They are often treated as "the truth" from those who hold them, even if the perception is inaccurate. This therefore makes them very powerful. Perceptions can be changed, although not easily, through honest dialogue and through changed behaviors.

TRUST AND CREDIBILITY

Increased trust in a leader results in increased credibility. Credibility is the currency required for a leader to have influence in the lives of others. When trust grows, a leader's credibility account grows with it. However, when trust declines, a leader's credibility account declines with it. In building and maintaining a credibility bank, we need to consider and understand seven key factors:

1. Our credibility bank is continually active even before we establish a relationship with a person or group. For example, when being interviewed for a new position, our credibility bank is influenced by such things as our reputation, credentials, and who is recommending us.

2. Our credibility bank belongs to us, but we don't have complete control over it, unlike our financial accounts where others need our authorization to impact or even access them. Others can make deposits or withdrawals based on what they say to third parties about their relationships and interactions with us.

3. Withdrawals (because of unfavorable behavior) are often greater in magnitude than deposits (for favorable behavior). Our mistakes or failures can potentially cost us more than we gain from successes. Research has shown that it takes five positive interactions to balance out one negative interaction. Our mistakes or failures can potentially cost us more than we gain from our successes.

4. The mere perception of how much credibility we have influences interactions we have with others. For instance, whether or not a proposal we're recommending gains support may hinge on how credible those considering it believe we are.

5. We can overdraw our credibility account to the point where it's next to impossible to restore. Bankruptcy has occurred. It's a situation so damaging that no amount of time or energy will likely restore it.

6. Our credibility can become so inflated that we get away with inappropriate behavior or mediocre performance. An example is the dynamic leader who spends little time preparing for meetings because colleagues readily accept his ideas based upon previously earned credibility.

7. Some things are worth losing our credibility for. Given the influence of pragmatism and utilitarianism in our society, we may resist sacrificing our credibility. However, core values drawn from the Bible should determine what is most important and what we should stand for, even at the cost of our credibility.

A LOOK AT THE 6 TRUST GAUGES
COMMUNICATION
Trust is facilitated by communication between people and groups. Sending clear messages and listening are the two primary mechanisms for effective communication. Sending clear messages reduces the potential for miscommunication while listening increases the likelihood of accurately hearing the message as well as shows respect to the sender.

Both the frequency and depth of conversations are important in cultivating and maintaining trust. For example, proximity of offices can significantly influence how often staff members talk with one another. Those members who come in contact often during the day or week have greater opportunity to dialogue. However, office doors that are often closed may communicate that you are not available or are too busy to talk.

Communication provides opportunity to:
- Explain and clarify expectations
- Seek feedback from others
- Share perceptions
- Test assumptions and ideas
- Disclose feelings
- Explain changes

Research has shown it is often through casual, unplanned social interaction that issues which can lead to distrust are resolved and perceptions are corrected or adjusted. Such communication can take place in unstructured meetings such as in a hallway, over a cup of coffee, or at lunch. However, other significant communication can be accomplished through structured gatherings such as staff meetings. This is why well designed and facilitated meetings are so important.

Additionally, self-disclosure can help to avoid misunderstandings. Self-disclosure is revealing some aspect of who you are, including thoughts, feelings, ideas, and fears. This practice can help prevent or correct others' misinterpretations of you.

Communication is vital to cultivating trust. When communication is limited or when leaders are not relational or accessible, people may begin to read into events, make assumptions, and ultimately distrust.

Reflective Questions for Communication

Do I personally seek to communicate clearly and regularly with those around me? How do I know?

Do we as an organization seek to communicate clearly and regularly with our constituents? How do we know?

CHARACTER

Character refers to a person's intrinsic value system and external actions. Areas often associated with character are honesty, fairness, and hard work. Proverbs 12:22 states, "The LORD detests lying lips, but he delights in men who are truthful." Trust is fostered when a person is perceived to be manifesting honesty in their communication and actions. It is both powerful and refreshing when those in leadership roles stand in front of a person or group and take responsibility for their actions. The simple phrase "I [or we] have made a mistake and take full responsibility for it" is seldom heard.

When people within a team or organization are not spending regular time together in communication, they may discover a decision has been made without their involvement. This may cause certain members to privately or publicly question the character of other members, even though those individuals may not have done anything unethical. In addition, when people say one thing and do another, or promise to do something but fail to follow through, their character can be called into question, resulting in an erosion of trust.

Credibility is established very simply. Tell people who you are or what you do. Then be that person and do what you have said you would do . . . In a simple sentence: Say what you mean and mean what you say.
– Dr. Frank Luntz, *Words That Work*

Since perceptions are held as truth, someone's character may be called into question even though they may not have committed any unethical act. Leaders must monitor the perceptions of others by regularly testing proposed actions before implementing them and by seeking honest feedback from others.

Reflective Questions for Character
Do I personally manifest honesty and integrity with those around me? How do I know?

Do we as an organization manifest honesty and integrity with our constituents? How do we know?

CONCERN

People tend to have confidence and trust in those who they perceive show authentic concern for them. In Philippians 2, Paul explains how we should imitate Christ in our actions and attitudes, including demonstrating concern for others.

Do nothing out of selfish ambition or vain conceit, but in humility consider others better than yourselves. Each of you should look not only to your own interests, but also to the interests of others.
– Philippians 2:3-4

Christian leaders have the task to manifest concern in three primary places: concern for self, concern for other members of the organization, and concern for the overall health and effectiveness of the organization. It is difficult to balance these three concerns. For example, executive compensation in many organizations has resulted in the employee perception that leadership is self-serving and not concerned about them and their needs. Also, the dismissal of someone may be interpreted as a lack of concern for that person even though it was actually important for the health of the organization.

In an attempt to either avoid giving negative feedback or to be merciful, Christian organizations sometimes either defer addressing performance problems with their personnel or provide mixed messages regarding their performance. However, when the problems become unbearable or begin to create unacceptable results, leadership sometimes attempts to intervene by either informing the person they will not advance any further in the organization or by dismissing them. By not addressing the issues early on, when the leadership "suddenly" takes action, it can be seen as harsh and unfeeling.

In cases like the one mentioned above, truth is necessary in order to help another person understand that his or her performance is not acceptable. However, the message needs to be delivered with a spirit of love and concern. Christians sometimes think they are manifesting love by not sharing the truth, when, in reality, they are only manifesting self-interest by avoiding the hard work of providing truthful feedback to someone.

Ephesians 4:15 instructs Christians to "speak the truth in love," defining this as a sign of Christian maturity. To bypass truth in the name of love, or to bypass love in the name of truth, falls short of this instruction and results in hurt.

Depending on how truth is communicated, the intervention may be perceived by the individual and others as uncaring due to limited previous feedback, hurt feelings, and even the loss of employment. Seldom do people initially view discipline or constructive feedback as a demonstration of genuine concern.

However, people are more likely to accept our feedback if they know we care about them.

Reflective Questions for Concern

Do I personally demonstrate concern and care for those around me? How do I know?

Do we as an organization demonstrate concern and care with our constituents? How do we know?

COMPETENCE

Competence is primarily concerned with an individual's or organization's capacity to perform a task or role with an acceptable level of proficiency. Sometimes people start in a position or role where they initially have the necessary competence to succeed. However, influences such as organizational growth, reduced personal energy level, personal problems, or cultural shifts can ultimately result in a decline in proficiency. When people's expectations regarding an organization's or individual's performance are not met, trust or confidence in that individual or organization can decline.

When people are perceived to be acting competently within their role, they are more likely to be viewed as trustworthy and are often granted greater credibility and opportunities to acquire positions of influence.

However, many people are not aware of how others perceive them. If someone does not know how they are perceived, they will have no idea if their performance is poor, sufficient, or even exceptional. In cases of poor competence, the individual may not realize that he or she is not measuring up. Reasons why people may not be aware of how others perceive them include:

- The individual does not solicit feedback from others.
- The individual does not understand the messages that are being sent.
- The individual will not accept the feedback they are given.
- The leader does not provide clear feedback.
- The leader does not have or use clearly defined performance standards .

To increase our self-awareness and make sure that we are performing proficiently:

1. We need to continually seek feedback on how others perceive we are performing.
2. We must always be sharpening our professional skills and learning new ones.
3. We need to be honest with ourselves and acknowledge when we are no longer gifted for a particular role.

Displaying such honesty and actions may encourage others to do the same and can lead to new levels of trust.

Reflective Questions for Competence

Do I personally demonstrate follow through and produce positive results? How do I know?

Do we as an organization demonstrate follow through and produce positive results? How do we know?

CONNECTEDNESS

Americans are spending a lot less time breaking bread with friends than we did twenty or thirty years ago.
– Robert Putnam, *Bowling Alone*

Relationships play a vital role in building and maintaining trust. When people are relationally connected to one another, they have a greater opportunity to know what is happening in the lives of others, to manifest care and concern when needs are discovered, and to keep potential for conflict and misunderstanding to a minimum.

An overarching theme in the Bible, explicitly stated in the book of Ecclesiastes, is that two are better than one. Confirming this, research conducted by the Gallup Organization, whose findings are presented in the book *Vital Friends*, showed that people who have a best friend at work are more likely to engage customers more effectively, get more done, have greater satisfaction with their job and pay, and be less likely to leave the company. Yet, relational connection in the U.S. has been on a 35 year decline. Research shows that we entertain fewer people in our homes and connect much less with neighbors than we did in the 50's-60's. A growing concern is that just when we are realizing the need for greater relational connection from leaders and employees, they may have fewer skills to even know how to form and sustain such relationships.

As we approach the new millennium, many of us modern crave men have acquired the things we need and are now burrowed into a socially detached style of unassisted living. Indeed, where our ancestors enjoyed the company of small groups, members of progressive societies are becoming monadic, foraging in the vicinity of other people but feeding mainly on themselves.
– John Locke, *The Devoicing of Society*

We sometimes have a propensity to use the way we "do relationships" with others as a standard of how others should "do relationships." However, we are all unique. Although not everyone has the exact same relational needs or relational resources, the following are universal principles essential for enhancing relational connection.

Heart. The "one another" commands found throughout the New Testament have, at their core, the assumption that we must first care enough about obeying God and building relational connections with others in order to risk even trying to build them. In addition, when people treat relationships in a utilitarian fashion, people get hurt.
"Friendships patterned on commodities, consumerism, mass production, and collectibles are friendships without heart. People were not designed to be treated as commodities, to be consumed, to be collected, or to have their relationships mass produced like assembly line goods. Such is a breeding ground for broken hearts."
–Len Davis, *Christ Centered Friendships*

Reciprocity. Reciprocity is an essential function of healthy relational connection. The basic tenant of this principle is: I will do something for you with the hope that you or someone else will do something for me when I need it. While this reciprocity should never be the heart motive for reaching out to others, it is a foundational aspect of most social relationships.
"If you don't go to somebody's funeral, they won't come to yours." –Yogi Berra
"Come to our breakfast, we'll come to your fire."
–Fire Dept. Slogan

Vulnerability. Vulnerability is sometimes confused with softness, especially by men. However, vulnerability is little more than sharing the truth about oneself at the appropriate time and with appropriate people. Vulnerability does require discernment, but it is not optional for building authentic relationships.

"As leaders increase in stature, a significant temptation draws them like a magnet. They are seduced into hiding the truth about themselves in order to create or maintain an image that they believe will maintain their influence. To maintain their position of leadership, people at the top may live lives of pretense and disguise, especially when faced with potential failure, which must be covered up at all costs in order to protect their authority and power. But it does not have to be this way." –Thrall, McNicol, McElrath, *The Ascent of a Leader*

Proximity. Proximity is the physical location of one person or group to another person or group. For example, you are more likely to have a closer relationship with someone you have regular contact with than with someone you do not. The person who works in your department, the neighbor who lives next door, and the friend you see regularly at church would all be examples. Proximity increases the amount of contact two individuals may have with one another.

"I have found over and over again how hard it is to be truly faithful to Jesus when I am alone. I need my brothers or sisters to pray with me, to speak with me about the spiritual task at hand, and to challenge me to stay pure in mind, heart, and body." –Henri Nouwen, *In the Name of Jesus*

Time. Time is related to how long you have known another person or group and how often you are with them. The longer you know someone, the more opportunities you have to interact, observe behavior, and express interest and concern about him or her.

Risk. "To involve oneself with another person for the purpose of ministry is risky. It requires that we concern ourselves with another's welfare rather than our own. Easy words. But vulnerable ministry offered to people who cannot be trusted to respond appreciatively is frightening, and when their response is neglect or rejection, the pain can be unbearable. Continued involvement at that point is the ultimate measure of love. Our Lord died for friends who rejected Him and for soldiers who beat Him."
–Larry Crabb, *Understanding People*

There is something powerful about relational connection. Without it, you will find increased conflict, misunderstanding, and distrust. With it, you will find greater joy, emotional health, and trust.

Reflective Questions for Connectedness
Do I personally seek to foster healthy relational connections with those around me? How do I know?

Do we as an organization foster an environment that values relational connection? How do we know?

CONSISTENCY

People tend to trust others who show predictability or consistency. When someone is erratic or unpredictable, we are less likely to trust him or her. For example, if a supervisor is friendly and joking around one day, the next day is angry and withdrawn, and another day is serious and reserved, people will develop a sense of uncertainty and begin to question the consistency of this leader. Consistency is also important in performance. How would you feel if, over the past year, the person responsible for producing financial reports for an organization provided some that were accurate and others that had errors? Such inconsistency would result in you second guessing his or her work, ultimately eroding the trust you have in him.

While none of us are 100% consistent, we must regularly assess if we are consistent enough in our words, actions, and performance to ensure a reasonable level of trust.

Reflective Questions for Consistency
Do I personally demonstrate consistency in my words, demeanor, and deeds? How do I know?

Do we as an organization demonstrate consistency with our customers? How do we know?

BALANCING THE 6 TRUST GAUGES
We can manage trust when we continually monitor communication, character, concern, connectedness, consistency, and competency. If distrust is detected between people or within the overall organization, it can most often be traced to the perceptions and expectations related to one or more of these six elements. Leaders face the daunting challenge of constantly balancing all six of the elements, even though attending to one may result in the perception that the others are being neglected. It's no wonder that cultivating and maintaining trust is such a challenge!

POSSIBLE SIGNS OF TRUST
- Regular time together as a team and with team members
- Problems addressed quickly and constructively
- Positive and enjoyable work environment
- Freedom and encouragement to question authority
- Mutual support for most significant decisions
- Atmosphere of care and concern for one another
- Information freely shared between people and groups

- Minimal suspicion regarding motives and decisions
- Deepening level of dialogue over time
- Long-term retention of employees and other constituents
- Regular, unscheduled opportunities for dialogue

POSSIBLE SIGNS OF BROKEN TRUST

- Excessive reliance on policies
- Fear of challenging authority
- Avoidance of difficult subjects
- Increased cliques
- Decreased social interaction
- Reduced enjoyment
- Second-guessing most decisions
- Increase of critical discussions behind closed doors
- Heavy dependence on hierarchal structures
- Atmosphere of suspicion and tension
- Intentionally withholding information
- Significant turnover of employees and other constituents

EXAMPLES OF BROKEN TRUST

There is no shortage of examples of broken trust in society, including many churches and organizations. The following is a list of examples of where trust has been broken, each with a different set of circumstances and magnitude of impact. The common elements for each example are broken expectations and disappointed people.

- A pastor who preaches on marital fidelity, while at the same time is having an affair
- A CEO who lays off employees, while accepting a lucrative salary and bonuses
- A politician who promises to reduce corruption is caught accepting bribes

- A denominational leader who challenges churches to follow Christ is convicted of stealing church funds
- A fundraiser who promises great returns to charitable organizations is arrested and bankrupt
- A manager who dismisses an employee without providing adequate feedback
- An employee who engages in political behavior and manipulation to accomplish their goals
- An employee who accepts a position at another organization without any discussion with current associates
- A person who fails to show up for a scheduled meeting
- A person who promises they will complete a task but never follows through

Each case of broken trust is influenced by perceptions and expectations held by the parties involved. Ultimately however, confidence is shaken resulting in an atmosphere of distrust, disappointment, cynicism, and difficulty trusting again.

REBUILDING BROKEN TRUST

When trust is broken, either for reasons of unethical behavior or due to differing expectations, the results are disappointment, hurt, and anger. It is very easy to respond by not wanting to trust again or invest the time and energy necessary to rebuild the lost trust. However, this only results in embedding unhealthy feelings and behaviors into the organization's culture.

Christian leaders must make trust a priority topic in their teams and organizations. The mission and performance of the organization will ultimately be limited or sacrificed without a culture of trust.

There are a variety of actions that need to be taken when attempting to rebuild broken trust:

1. Learn. Have each member of your leadership team read this chapter on trust. This will create a common working knowledge and language related to the theme of trust.

2. Reflect. As a leader, reflect upon your own willingness to learn about how your actions may contribute to a culture of distrust. Questions could include:
- How did the trust get broken?
- What assumptions was I making?
- What were my expectations?
- Were my expectations understood?
- Were my expectations realistic?
- What would Jesus do at this point?

3. Conduct a trust audit. Identify the primary sources that have contributed to the distrust. The 6 Trust Gauges can be a helpful tool to accomplish this. During this time, it is vital to suspend fault-finding. Be solution focused, not fault focused. The goal is mutual understanding where all parties need to agree to what has contributed to the distrust. But this does not necessarily require agreement. Even if another person or group was the primary contributor to the broken trust, energy must be targeted towards answering the question: "What is the appropriate action that will lead to rebuilding trust?"

4. Forgive often. Without forgiveness, it is unlikely that trust will be rebuilt since previous failures to live up to your expectations will cloud the rebuilding process. Without forgiveness, the breach of trust can consume enormous amounts of emotional energy and lead to a cynical spirit.

Bear with each other and forgive whatever grievance you may
have against one another. Forgive as the Lord forgave you.
– Colossians 3:13

Forgiving does not necessarily mean forgetting, but rather
putting the offense behind you and moving on with a positive
attitude.

5. Model confidentiality. When trust is broken, fear and
anxiety levels are usually raised between the parties involved.
It is of utmost importance to create an environment where
participants know that what is said will not leave the room. For
this to happen, the smaller the group, the better.

6. Create safety. When people feel threatened, they are not
likely to be receptive to feedback or to sharing honestly about
their own perceptions and what contributed to them. Safety
is produced by confidentiality, non-attacking communication,
and demonstrating genuine concern.

7. Develop expectations. For distrust to change to trust,
people must work towards agreed upon expectations and
seek to live up to them. This should result in a plan of action to
address any concrete factors that contributed to the distrust.
For example, if lack of communication is a factor, create new
communication opportunities and channels. If competency is a
factor, determine how skills can be sharpened.

8. Seek assistance. When necessary, bring in an outside
facilitator to assist you with identifying and solving trust issues.
Sometimes, an outside voice or neutral party can see processes
that those closest to the issues cannot see.

9. Plan for disappointment. It is important to understand there will be many more disappointments ahead. Using a sound biblical anthropology, accept the fact that disappointment is a normal part of life. You will let others down, and others will let you down. God uses disappointment to teach us, discipline us, and to point us to heaven – a place where there will be no more disappointments!

10. Healthy departure. Sometimes it is necessary for a person to leave a team or organization because the level of distrust has resulted in complete destruction of credibility. However, such cases should never be the norm since they cause repercussions to the organization and its members. In such cases, all parties should invest the time necessary to learn from the situation, and the organization must strive to demonstrate love and concern towards the individual who needs to leave. When handled appropriately, this can ultimately result in a fresh start for all parties involved.

SUMMARY
Christian leaders must make culture management a part of their primary role. Remember, it is much easier to work towards retaining trust than to rebuild it. A trust-friendly culture will make the work environment more healthy and effective for everyone involved. ◼

CASE STUDY ON TRUST

NOTE: The following case study is designed to serve as a tool for a group or team to discuss the dynamics of trust in an organization.

John, Sue, Ron, and Steve work together as a church staff at First Church, a ministry of 400. John is the founder of the 15 year old church and serves as senior pastor while Sue, Ron, and Steve serve in a variety of associate staff roles. Ron and Sue have a growing frustration with John's leadership, including the amount of time he spends with Steve and the amount of time he is away from the church. They also have a growing concern over the quality of his preaching and his desire to be involved in all of the church decisions, even related to their areas of responsibility.

John likes Ron and Sue but feels like they are not following through on what he believes needs to happen in the church. He sometimes feels they continually challenge his authority by the questions they ask. John sometimes feels that Ron would like to take his place as the senior pastor and also questions Ron's allegiance to him and to the church. John dreads holding staff meetings because of the discomfort he feels due to these issues.

1. Check which of the "Possible Signs of Broken Trust" are present.

☐ Excessive reliance on policies   ☐ Decreased social interaction
☐ Fear of challenging authority   ☐ Second-guessing most decisions
☐ Increased cliques   ☐ Atmosphere of suspicion and tension
☐ Reduced enjoyment   ☐ Intentionally withholding information
☐ Avoidance of difficult subjects   ☐ Dependence on hierarchal structures
☐ Increase of critical discussions   ☐ Significant turnover of employees
　 behind closed doors   　 and other constituents

2. Using the 6 Trust Gauges, discuss what may have contributed to the distrust of this team.

3. What questions would you ask the group and individuals?

4. What are possible outcomes if this team does not address issues related to distrust? What can they do to rebuild the trust?

//

TRUST AUDIT EXERCISE

Make a copy of this Audit Questionnaire. Complete one audit on yourself and ask another team member to complete one on you.

Individually, reflect upon what, if any, discrepancies exist between your assessment of yourself and how others see you. Why may these exist?

As a pair or group, spend time reviewing your audits. Are there discrepancies between how the members of the group view the trust/distrust level? If so, why might this difference exist?

Character 1   2   3   4   5
speaking truthfully and acting with integrity   *Why this rating?*

Communication 1   2   3   4   5
sharing information regularly with others   *Why this rating?*

Connectedness 1   2   3   4   5
spending time with others   *Why this rating?*

Concern 1   2   3   4   5
showing genuine love for and interest in others   *Why this rating?*

Competence 1   2   3   4   5
demonstrating skill in what you do   *Why this rating?*

Consistency 1   2   3   4   5
manifesting predictability and reliability   *Why this rating?*

What signs of trust and distrust do you believe are present in the relationship or organization at this time?

What can be done to cultivate a culture of trust in your organization?

RESOURCES

Badaracco, J., Ellsworth, R. (1989). *Leadership and the Quest for Integrity*. Cambridge: Harvard Business School Press.

Block, P. (1993). *Stewardship*. San Francisco: Barrett Kohler.

Bok, S. (1989). *Lying*. New York: Vintage.

Greenleaf, R. (1977). *Servant Leadership*. New York: Paulist Press.

Handy, C. (1993). *Understanding Organizations*. New York: Oxford Press.

Heifetz, R. (1994). *Leadership without Easy Answers*. Cambridge: Harvard University Press.

Hybels, B. (1993). *Descending into Greatness*. Grand Rapids: Zondervan.

Kelly, R. (1992). *The Power of Followership*. New York. Currency/Doubleday.

Kouzes, M., Posner, B. (1993). *Credibility*. San Francisco: Jossey-Bass.

Kramer, R., Tyler, T. (1996). *Trust in Organizations*. Thousand Oaks: Sage.

Lucas, J. (1998). *Balance of Power*. New York: AMACOM.

O'Toole, J. (1995). *Leading Change*. San Francisco: Jossey-Bass.

Quinn, R. (1996). *Deep Change*. San Francisco: Jossey-Bass.

Rath, T. (2006). *Vital Friends*. Gallup Press.

Rath, T. and O. Clifton (2004). *How Full is Your Bucket?* Gallup Press

Reddy, W. B. (1994). *Intervention Skills*. San Diego: Pfeiffer.

Sande, K. (1997). *The Peacemaker*. Grand Rapids: Baker Books.

Schein, E. (1992). *Organizational Culture and Leadership*. San Francisco: Jossey-Bass.

Shaw, R. B. (1997). *Trust in the Balance*. San Francisco: Jossey-Bass.

Sonnenberg, F. (1994). *Managing with a Conscience*. New York: McGraw Hill.

Wagner and Harter (2006). *12: The Elements of Great Managing*. Gallup Press.

Waldroop and Butler (2000). *The 12 Bad Habits that Hold Good People Back*. Currency Doubleday.

TO HANDLE YOURSELF,
USE YOUR HEAD;
TO HANDLE OTHERS,
USE YOUR HEART.

ELEANOR ROOSEVELT

CHAPTER THREE

MAKING RELATIONAL GLUE

UNDERSTANDING THE IMPORTANCE OF EQ
BY DAVID A. MARKS, D.Min.

Reflections of an emotionally aware leader:

I was finally able to retire after what I considered to be a long and successful career. Looking back on the myriad of people I worked with in those 42 years, a few stood out above the rest, and one in particular caught my attention. His name was Clark, and he served as a mid-level manager in the company where I was a VP of Sales. Peers often referred to Clark as having extraordinary "people skills" or "soft skills."

Now with time to reflect, I began to identify those specific characteristics that made him different and put him in a class of his own. My initial thought was that he just naturally possessed a high-likeability type personality AND he was highly effective in his work. Because of these two traits, others sought him out which made him popular among both the blue-collar workers and the white-shirt types like me. Ultimately, I realized the "secret sauce" Clark possessed was much more than his inborn temperament traits. He had intentionally developed his ability to make relational glue (emotional intelligence). He had somehow broken free of the chains of self-doubt and ego-mania and was liberated to see others for who they really were. That was it! We trusted Clark because he could objectively assess himself and others. Without lots of drama and emotional thrashing, he could give good advice and make wise decisions while motivating and making others feel valued in the process.

BIOLOGY MEETS LEADERSHIP THEORY

Neuroscientists and organizational theorists have come to refer to the Clark factor described in the story above as **Emotional Intelligence** (EQ/EI) or **Social Intelligence**. Unlike IQ which is established at birth and in early childhood and changes only slightly throughout life, EQ can be acquired and be significantly developed. Additionally, researchers in behavioral neuroscience have made stunning discoveries about how our brain cells actually create a chemical connection with others. This is measurably true between leaders and their followers. A leader's mood drives the mood of the team. Leaders who consistently manifest emotional maturity will likely have a high performing and loyal team following them.

I like to think of EQ as "relational glue" because the test of high emotional intelligence is ultimately seen in our ability to cultivate and sustain meaningful relationships. This relational glue is maximized by mixing the most recognized attributes of EQ.

THE 5 MOST RECOGNIZED ATTRIBUTES OF EQ

1. Self-Awareness. Self-Awareness is a foundational element. Individuals who understand themselves are able to leverage their strengths and minimize their weaknesses. There is a freedom from "self" that comes with honest self-assessment. Not surprisingly, those who possess high EQ inevitably pursue additional insight about how they are wired. Then, they make appropriate adjustments to their thinking and behaviors and move on. Confidence grows and the fear of weaknesses being discovered by others fades.

Ask Yourself: What have I learned about myself recently?
Try: Use this chapter to identify five areas where you can begin to grow as an EQ Leader.

2. Self-Management. Self-Management is the proactive solution-based response to good feedback. A non-defensive attitude to problems contributes to trustworthiness in the midst of confusion, conflict, and change. The ability to redirect reactive impulses (such as an angry outburst, powering up, and blame shifting) into a stable response that explores solutions builds deep trust in a team.

Ask Yourself: In what areas do I have knowledge about myself that I could act on in order to improve my EQ Leadership?
Try: Consider reducing "learning time" and intentionally adding some "acting time."

3. Passion. Passion for the task turns work into fuel for life. The work is energizing in itself. Remove passion from the challenges of life, and stress and anxiety will soon replace contentment. A motivated person is like a race horse in the gate waiting for the bell to ring. Their internal compass points them towards an attitude of optimism and of hope, believing every day holds a new challenge and a new opportunity to contribute something of value.

Ask Yourself: Is my self-talk more pessimistic or optimistic?
Try: "Thank You" therapy (intentionally focusing on things you appreciate in others and situations, events, or things for which you are thankful).
Note: Pessimism is frequently generated by fear without hope.

4. Empathy. Empathy is the heart of EQ, literally. At the core of high EQ is relatability. When you are able to think like others and feel what they are experiencing, you will be able to coach and develop them. People around you are able to perceive that you "get" them; they are convinced you really care. With such trust, they will let you into the inner sanctum of their lives. They do not fear a judgmental attitude, and they believe you have their best interest in view. By contrast, leaders who have an easily-bruised ego will seldom be given the opportunity to shape the heart of an individual. Loyalty to such leaders contributes to an employee's personal satisfaction and thus their longevity with the company.

>*Ask Yourself: How well do I know the people I work closest with? Can I name the top concerns or burdens they bear outside of their work demands?*
>
>*Try: Send a note, make a call, or demonstrate personal interest in someone this week.*

5. Connections. Connections come easily to the possessors of EQ. Such leaders are tuned in to themselves and others, and as a result, they are frequently known as networkers par excel 'lance. The inherent trust in these leaders gives credence to their recommendations. They are able to lead positive change with greater ease because their power to persuade others is directly linked to the strong "relational glue" they have made while developing EQ skills.

>*Ask Yourself: Is your circle of friends getting smaller and weaker or stronger and deeper?*
>
>*Try: Commit to a date to connect with someone.*

WATCHING THE RAINMAKERS IN ACTION

Because EQ Leaders have sharpened their ability to recognize and manage their own emotions maturely, they experience the benefits of being considered approachable by others. As a result of those growing connections, the EQ Leader gets opportunities to have significant influence in arenas that aren't open for those who are skilled but secluded. Studies have shown that people with increased EQ are, more often than not, ahead of their lower EQ counter parts in:

- Personal sense of well-being (less depression & anxiety)
- Problem solving
- Being viewed as leaders
- Being trusted by others
- Having higher incomes
- Being promoted in work responsibilities more often
- Having more opportunities and invitations to be on a team

   (Goleman, Boyatzis, and Mckee in *Primal Leadership: The Hidden Driver of Great Performance*)

I call these people "rainmakers." They make things happen through their many connections. These connections are more than just informational or structural. They are drawn together by a common thread of mutual respect and trust with others who manage resources and are responsible for making decisions. The benefits are hard to measure perfectly, but the positive effect on EQ Leaders is undeniable.

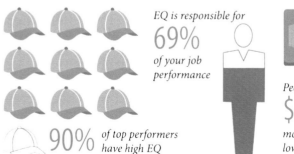

EQ is responsible for
69%
of your job performance

90% *of top performers have high EQ*

People with high EQ make
$29,000
more annually than their low EQ counterparts

Information from talentsmart.com

7 RESULTS AND BENEFITS OF HAVING HIGH EQ

The following are seven observations I have made about emotionally intelligent leaders. They consistently and intuitively do these things in order to be healthy leaders and to encourage relational glue among their team members.

1. THEY TAKE OFF THEIR MASK

It's okay to just be you. The standard is growth, not perfection. EQ thrives in the world of reality and truth. Pretenders have to hide because the notion of transparency is threatening to the image they have created and are trying to maintain. The insecure leader has a well-honed, subjective filter to scan any incoming comments, decisions, and actions through the mask of self-preservation. In order to protect themselves from anything that casts them in an undesirable light, they can become chameleons, changing their behaviors to react to the perceived challenge. Such leaders often manifest a passive-aggressive style of leadership. This insulation to vulnerability will likely prevent others from giving the type of honest feedback that is needed for leaders to grow their EQ. However, vulnerability needs to come with discernment. Emotionally intelligent leaders are able to assess the situation and share appropriately while avoiding the act of oversharing.

2. THEY ARE OPEN TO ASSESSMENT AND FEEDBACK

Proper assessment can bring clarity to the leader regarding his or her capabilities, compatibilities, and capacities for leadership and work. Since no one has the "whole package" of gifts and abilities, we are wise to discern what strengths and weaknesses we naturally bring to the leadership table. We highly recommend that leaders who want to grow in emotional intelligence arrange an externally-facilitated Leader 360 Feedback Process which includes gathering anonymous perspectives of how others see you as a leader. These perspectives include your own view of yourself and also the views of your supervisor(s), your peers, and those who report to you. We cannot grow without feedback because it identifies strengths, bad behaviors, and possible blind spots. Leadership maturity does not occur in a vacuum; we need accurate and personal input from others so we can appropriately define who we are and who we are not. Show me a person who is easily offended, justifies their actions when questioned, and deflects blame on to others, and I will show you a pygmy leader.

3. THEY ACT ACCORDING TO WHO THEY ARE

A common characteristic in high functioning leaders is their ability to establish boundaries that are consistent with their own leadership DNA. They have decided what they will and will not do. They do not waste their time and effort trying to do something or be something they were never intended to do or be. Instead, they pour their concentrated effort into developing the person they are, not what others think they should be.

Do not think of yourself more highly than you ought, but rather think of yourself with sober judgment… – Romans 12:3

4. THEY ARE INTENTIONAL ABOUT WHO SURROUNDS THEM

Who is on your team? The answer to that question depends on which team we are talking about. Ideally, we should each have a minimum of two teams.

The first team you should build is an unofficial team of personal truth-tellers. This team is willing to say the hard things in a skillful way. In the Bible, Ephesians 4:15 tells us to "speak the truth in love." This team of encouragers may be from within or from outside your organization. They can be mentors, coaches, or friends. The most important thing is to have regular contact with these types of people. Conventional leadership wisdom would say every leader should have one and be one.

Pity the leader caught between unloving critics and uncritical lovers. – The late John Gardener, Scholar, Presidential Advisor

Better is open rebuke than hidden love. Wounds from a friend can be trusted, but an enemy multiplies kisses…
– Proverbs 27:5-6

A second team you should invest in is your work team. GREAT teams don't happen accidentally; they require focused intentionality. The key is to be able to synergize using relational connections more than relying on positional power as discussed in Chapter 1. Increasing the understanding of EQ among team members will help produce more satisfying and productive results. Simply doing popular "team building events" will yield only limited benefits if used without the concepts of EQ being embedded. Try designing an interactive training exercise for your team to begin to understand the key concepts of EQ. You might be surprised by how many illustrations they can come up with to demonstrate when EQ is/isn't working.

5. THEY CREATE ENVIRONMENTS OPEN TO NEW IDEAS

A notable benefit for individuals and teams with a high EQ is the freedom to plow and pursue new ideas without fear of rejection. Relational glue fuels the bold exploration of the new and better. A contagious optimism and belief that "nothing is impossible" infiltrates the entire ethos of such teams. They are unintimidated by the inevitable failures that accompany great successes. Without strong relational glue, there is a natural resistance to sharing knowledge, skills, and power. Self-preservation will win every time if key members of the team feel threatened by conflict or if someone is always pulling rank.

Mature leaders have nothing to prove; their egos have been trained not to react defensively when dissenting opinions surface. They listen, they learn, and then they lead. They rely on the safety net of their network. Risk becomes both fun and rewarding. Data contrary to their first opinions is welcomed. They fully embrace shifts in thinking that may ultimately dismantle their own ideas. Why? Because they are secure with whom they are, and they have built relationships that are sustained by trust.

6. THEY HELP SUSTAIN MOMENTUM

Creating momentum in an organization is for a catalyst what catching a big wave is to a world-class surfer. They see it coming in the distance and they have the right sense of timing and skill to take it for a nice ride. However, many catalysts do NOT possess strong EQ skills which many believe are essential to sustain real change. EQ Leaders may or may not be catalytic in their leadership, but the best and the brightest know that lasting positive change will not happen without someone who possesses the expertise in reading and relating well to the ones who will be responsible to implement the change. Additionally, EQ Leaders are constantly nourishing the relationships in their expanding network; they may more readily become aware of errors to avoid. Perhaps you have noticed that when momentum is reinforced with relational glue, problems are resolved more easily, diversions into the trivial are less frequent, recruiting volunteers for the cause is easier, resources are gathered faster, and celebrations are needed more often as milestones are reached more quickly.

The wise see trouble coming long before it comes and takes action, but the unaware keep going and pay the price.
– Based on Proverbs 27:12

7. THEY TAKE TIME FOR REFLECTION

Every high quality electric model train has a vital piece of track called the re-railer. When the train passes over that particular piece of track, the wheels are realigned for the next smooth trip around the Christmas tree. By the time the train returns, it is starting to wobble again, but as it passes over the re-railer, it gets recalibrated and keeps on going.

Lest you think that high performing leaders are driven by endless activity and metrics, be assured that the sustainability of leaders requires time for reflection and recalibration. Show me a leader that is able to show empathy, deepen friendships, and contribute to important networks, and I will show you a leader who understands the importance of contemplation and self-reflection. You can't give away what you don't have. Keep your reservoirs full.

HOW EQ WORKS

I like to refer to the practice of EQ as the Zorro Effect. Like the masked swordsman who left his mark wherever he went, so it is with the high EQ Leader. They leave a mark on the lives they touch. When I am explaining this process to our clients at The Center, I like to make the noise of a sword slicing through the air making the Z pattern. Try it! It's addictive and a great reminder of how EQ naturally flows from self-awareness, to self-management, to understanding others, and to making relational glue.

The Zorro Effect

Only those with good **self-awareness** can properly self-manage their known strengths and weaknesses. Good **self-management** allows an individual to be free from needing to filter everything through the grid of ego and self-esteem, and therefore, allows them to manifest genuine interest in others, showing empathy and providing encouragement. Only when you **understand others** can you make an informed investment into their lives and **grow the relationship** in the right directions for the right reasons. **Z**

GETTING STARTED ON DEVELOPING YOUR EQ
1. TRAIN YOUR BRAIN
With intentionality and proper techniques, it is possible to train

your brain! EQ can be learned, but not in the conventional way normal cognitive learning takes place. Different parts of the brain are responsible for different types of learning.

- The **limbic system** is the area of the brain that manages our motivations, imaginations, and is the processing area for our myriad of emotions, including empathy.
- The **neocortex** area of the brain governs the analytical, sequential, and technical aspects of learning. Training seminars work well on the neocortex but not on the limbic.
- The **reptilian function** of the brain is the operational core where our most basic non-voluntary instincts reside.
- **Plasticity** is the term neurologists use to describe the gradual building of a neurological bridge between the RATIONAL brain and the EMOTIONAL brain.

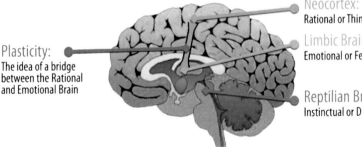

Neocortex:
Rational or Thinking Brain

Limbic Brain:
Emotional or Feeling Brain

Plasticity:
The idea of a bridge between the Rational and Emotional Brain

Reptilian Brain:
Instinctual or Dinosaur Brain

Literally billions upon billions of microscopic neurons form over time to increase the speed by which the rational and emotional centers of the brain swap information. To train your brain to be more EQ proficient, you must promote the building and strengthening of the neurological bridge by "feeding" both the rational (neocortex) and the emotional (limbic). Information alone is insufficient. One can read about EQ in a book or attend a training seminar on the subject and still remain virtually unchanged EVEN IF he or she believed absolutely everything that was taught! Why? Because the limbic system is not activated by knowledge. The emotional center needs to experience the feelings associated with being relationally connected with others. This is why EQ is so dependent on honest feedback from others. Start with yourself first and TRAIN YOUR BRAIN.

2. PICK AND PRACTICE EQ SKILLS

EQ skills are best developed by focusing on one or two at a time and practicing them until they start to come naturally. Using the following chart, select one trait and start practicing the higher EQ behaviors listed. Note the effect it has on you and on others. This is not simply an academic exercise but rather a bridge-building effort to get the rational and emotional centers of your brain talking to each other using the same language.

PRACTICE   FAIL   PRACTICE   IMPROVE   PRACTICE   MASTER   PRACTICE   DEVELOP OTHERS

EQ TRAITS	LOWER EQ BEHAVIORS	HIGHER EQ BEHAVIORS
Accessibility	Cocoons/Isolates himself, has a closed door policy that sends the message, "Can't you see I'm very busy because I'm very important." Brushes people off when bothered.	Lots of traffic around this person's office. Others like to drop by. The door is usually open; a kind and encouraging word awaits those who enter. Predictably available.
Active listening	Is easily distracted while others are talking. Maintains poor eye contact, hands are busy with phone, pens, or paper. Interrupts or changes subjects abruptly.	Maintains good eye contact, leans toward and not away from those speaking. Smiles naturally, nodding in agreement, does not interrupt or dominate the conversation.

EQ TRAITS	LOWER EQ BEHAVIORS	HIGHER EQ BEHAVIORS
Attunement	Can appear out of sync with the team. Is often viewed as disconnected, aloof, or myopic. Personal irritations dominate thoughts and therefore limit the ability to value others or focus on the larger issues.	Can read the room very well. Sees the big picture and can stay focused on personal and professional priorities. Intuitively moves towards synergy with the team rather than isolation.
Communication	Talks and then thinks. Speaks up even when it won't help. Slow to return emails and phone calls.	Thinks before talking. Only speaks when doing it helps the situation. Keeps lines of communication open even when frustrated. Returns phone calls, emails, and texts promptly. Follows through on promises made. Generates progress reports frequently.
Conflict	Being "right" is more important than relationships. Is willing to sacrifice "Esprit De Corps" (group loyalty/ spirit) in order to make a point. Must have the last word. Often makes normal conflict feel like a personal attack. Overly sensitive and subjective.	Remains calm and level-headed. Encourages healthy conflict. Delights in truth spoken with empathy. Believes conflict can strengthen relationships.
Developing Others	Stands by "every man for himself" and "I paid my dues so now it's time for you to do the same." Seldom views himself as a mentor, nor is he/she highly sought for the role.	Reads others well and spots potential quickly. Feels no anxiety about helping others with the "tricks of the trade." Usually has been coached and knows the value of helping others.
Empathy	Treats people all the same or treats them according to what he/she wants from them. Self-serving and preferential.	Treats people as individuals and can identify with their emotional wants, needs, fears, and dreams.

EQ TRAITS	LOWER EQ BEHAVIORS	HIGHER EQ BEHAVIORS
Framing	Generally has a more negative "half-empty" view of life and problems. Assumes the worst case scenario and has trouble trusting others. Tends to leap to negative conclusions.	Generally has a more positive "half-full" view of life and problems. Sees challenges as opportunities and seeks to inspire others.
Friendliness	Will return the obligatory "hello" if someone else initiates it. Does not go out of the way to engage or greet others. Tends to want others to see him or her as hard working and serious.	Lights up, smiles, and diverts from the task-at-hand to warmly acknowledge others who enter his/her space. Approachable. Happy to help out or answer questions.
Humor	Seldom shares something light-hearted with the group. Does not seem amused by the stories and jokes of others. Comes across as serious most of the time. Is easily annoyed if he/she sees co-workers enjoying something non-work related.	Often heard laughing. Uses self-deprecating humor. Enjoys healthy banter with the team. Enjoys hearing and telling stories.
Mood Management	Allows people and situations to control his/her emotions resulting in irritability and ambivalence in decisions. Example: "You MADE me so mad I can't think straight…" Conversely, may deny that emotions impact his/her thinking or cloud judgment at all. Broods when emotions lead his/her judgment. May have outbursts, make threats, or use highly dramatic statements.	Identifies and owns his/her emotions. Does not view emotions as good or bad but rather as indicators requiring action. Displays emotions that are congruent with the espoused values of the group. Can easily recognize when other people are affecting his/her emotional state.

EQ TRAITS	LOWER EQ BEHAVIORS	HIGHER EQ BEHAVIORS
Passion/ Motivation	Pursues primarily extrinsic rewards. Finds little enduring satisfaction in doing a task for the sake of the task.	Has passion for the work that goes beyond money and status. Motivated by the thrill of the hunt.
Problem Solving	Reacts towards people. Looks for someone to blame. May try and control the situation or withdraw completely.	Responds to complications. Sees trouble coming before it arrives. Likes to solve problems collaboratively. Comfortable with blameless resolution.
Relationships/ Connections	Tends to have surface friendships. Has a mysterious side and privacy is very important. Most relationships outside the immediate family are utilitarian. Can act passive-aggressive to assure others do not get too close. Can easily focus only on tasks and invest little in personal relationships. Leaves meetings quickly when they have concluded.	Builds networks of people that are both deep and wide. Naturally works to connect others and liberally shares information, resources, and ideas with them. Lingers after meetings to converse and catch-up. An open door policy is a norm. Intentionally makes rounds in the office to check-in and keep relationships from becoming too distant.
Self-Awareness	Does not interpret nonverbal messages well. Blind spots go undetected and feedback is viewed as punishing. Seems oblivious to tensions in the room. Casts an image of himself that he wants others to see him in.	Has an accurate assessment of self and is secure in assigning proper weight factors to personal strengths and weaknesses. Seeks input. Models transparency and vulnerability appropriately.
Self-Regulation	May have a victim mentality or a defeatist attitude relative to personal or organizational changes. Prefers the status quo. Suspicious of others and uses defensive routines to ward off personal criticism or new requirements.	Arrests impulses and alters mood and perspectives to make positive changes that will maximize strengths and mitigate elements that hinder performance and limit relationships.

EQ TRAITS	LOWER EQ BEHAVIORS	HIGHER EQ BEHAVIORS
Social Skills	Awkward. Feels anxious around others. May over compensate by talking too much, too little, or too loud. Does not understand reciprocity in conversations.	Gives friendly and warm greetings. Smiles frequently, initiates conversation, and makes others feel valued. "Friendliness with a purpose."
Stress Management	Frequently feels overloaded and overwhelmed. Has difficulty staying organized. Low level panic resides just below the surface. Restlessness when away from the office. May try to self-medicate.	Has enough self-awareness to know how and when to recharge. Adjusts schedule to match natural personal rhythms. Finds fulfillment in his/her work and does not fret about segregating work from his personal life. Practices self-care through gracious exercise of boundaries. Seldom procrastinates.
Teamwork	Shows annoyance with the need for meetings. Prefers to work alone and then combine ideas if it becomes absolutely necessary. Frequently is late for meetings or seems distracted by fiddling with his/her phone or papers during the meetings. Often guarded or leery of the motives of others on the team.	Gives and seeks good feedback to stimulate the team's growth. Demonstrates trust in team members. Provides balanced doses of inspiration, encouragement, and accountability. Pulls a fair share of the work load and quickly recognizes the efforts of others to do the same.
Thoughtful Questions	Asks loaded questions revealing hidden agenda or preference. Puts people on the spot but is defensive when challenged by others. Won't let things go… keeps asking the same old question with new words.	Possesses strong critical thinking skills. Can play the devil's advocate role by throwing cold water on the ideas of others. Asks good clarifying questions.
Use of Power	Relies on POSITIONAL power.	Relies on RELATIONAL power.

3. EXPERIMENT WITH A VARIETY OF LEADERSHIP "HATS"

In this chapter, we have been talking about EQ Leaders in order to describe a particular kind of leader. Obviously, not everyone who has high EQ is a leader in an organization, nor does every leader possess EQ. Succumbing to the pressure within the leadership culture to be "consistent" (always the same) may come at a cost for the EQ Leader. Many leaders rightly resist the idea of being labeled with one of the traditional "pigeon holes" associated with trait leadership. Generalized titles such as laissez-faire, autocratic, authoritarian, charismatic, transformational, or servant-leader may capture a leader's default style in normal conditions, but they can also feel too constraining when dealing with the large spectrum of people on your team. However, high EQ leaders are terrific at reading people in their current context of need and can easily morph into the style that is needed at the moment. For instance, there are some great advantages to being an "autocratic leader," but if the manager remains consistently autocratic even when the situation calls for a large dose of empathy, trust may be lost with that team member.

If you are like me, you have a variety of hats for the different seasons of the year. I try not to wear my over-the-ears wool hat during the summer heat wave, but I am glad to have it when shoveling snow. Likewise, EQ leaders need to wear a variety of hats depending on the season of their organization. **A high EQ leader will know when is best to put on each different hat.**

The Coaching Hat. Wear this hat to help build up your team by recognizing their underutilized talents and connecting them with new opportunities to help surface and shine those abilities. This personal approach can be motivating and stretching, benefiting both the individual and the organization.

The Delegation Hat. Wear this hat when it is essential to let your team wrestle with problems and generate new ideas. The Delegation Hat lets you intentionally step out of the role of decision leader and entrusts some high level discussions and decisions to your team. Your team will feel valued and invested in the process.

The Pacesetting Hat. Wear this hat to motivate by modeling. Put it on and jump in! When there is a big goal or the team needs to pull together quickly for a project, the pacesetter sets both the pace and the priority by digging in on the front lines. He/she is no longer just motivating and encouraging from a distance. While this is not a good long-term strategy, it does create comradery and also puts some of the poor performers on notice that more is expected at times. It is always good for a quick win.

The Captain Hat. Wear this hat when a take-charge, autocratic leader is needed. This can be a welcomed voice when things have become chaotic or a group has lost its bearings and is mired in a sea of opinions. Generally speaking, if you must keep reminding people that you are in charge, you're not! It is amazing how a firm tone used sparingly and in the right setting can instantly pull a team back together. Low EQ Leaders struggle with this because they are either tripping over their own ego (power tripping) or they are too timid because of the fear of falling into disfavor with others.

The Dream Hat. Every worthy cause begins with a vision of something better. Wear this hat to encourage creativity and new ideas. Eyes that look are common; eyes that SEE are rare. Through the fog, through the smoke, and through the darkness, visionaries emerge. When an EQ Leader puts on the

Dream Hat, things are about to change. They see the summit and they get excited about getting there. Their inspirational powers create excitement; their personal rapport invites others to join the journey. Too many dreams and too little execution and the Dream Hat does more harm than good. Used wisely, it invigorates the team and inspires innovation.

4. BRINGING OTHERS ALONG FOR THE RIDE

There is a fantastic linkage between mastering EQ qualities and passing them on to others who are ready for the journey. Follow this logic: the only ones who can  truly transfer these skills are the people who have them. These people have acquired the skills by learning from those who possessed them and modeled them well. I experienced this firsthand nearly two decades ago when I first meet Jay Desko, Ph.D., in graduate school where he was one of the deans and a professor. This was my initial exposure to the concepts of EQ and the soft skills needed for effective leadership. Now after years of working with him and others on our team who consistently and intuitively integrate EQ with proven leadership traits, I see just how fundamentally important EQ is to the art and science of leadership.

The good news is EQ can be learned, but not without an increased knowledge base of it and a strong commitment to practice. It has always amused me that the best athletes in the world still have coaches. I remember hearing Tiger Woods in his prime talking about "his coach." Watching 300-pound NFL linemen being coached by a 175-pound coach cracks me up. BUT it does show that the best continue to be coached. If you are going to help others, make sure you are continuing to get help to move to the next level of EQ development.

5. LEARN TO READ THE BEHAVIOR OF OTHERS

Humans are very complex! Commingling emotion, personality, temperament, intellect, and the motivations of the heart can make understanding what someone really wants hard to decipher. Having finely honed EQ skills allows a leader to read the source of frustration in others and give them what they actually need in order to once again be happily engaged and productive. The following examples show how leaders can help ease tension by paying close attention to how their employees are acting.

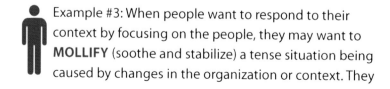 Example #1: When people are trying to shape their context by focusing on tasks, they are trying to **MANAGE**. They want more authority to direct resources in order to accomplish more tasks. Allow them to manage. Increase their responsibility slightly, and give them more authority to make decisions and impact change. Don't try to restrict them or micromanage them.

Example #2: When people are focused on shaping the contest for others, they are trying to **MOTIVATE**. Generally, this type of person is going to be excited, and filled with all kinds of new ideas. They want to inspire you and motivate you to do something new. Get excited with them and lean into their ideas. Don't stifle their creativity and interest in others. Motivate them in return to stay focused on the tasks at hand, but give them a bit of margin to explore the next steps in fleshing out the details of their ideas.

Example #3: When people want to respond to their context by focusing on the people, they may want to **MOLLIFY** (soothe and stabilize) a tense situation being caused by changes in the organization or context. They want long-term adjustments in the organization to positively affect others. Share their concern by showing empathy. Don't pressure them into agreement, but assure them that changes are not being made without thought and consideration as to how it will affect others.

Example #4: When people want to respond to their context by focusing on the tasks, they may want to **MANDATE** the behavior of others by applying metrics and data as the "proof" that they are right. Although few decisions can be based strictly on sterile data, the EQ Leader will allow them to do the analysis and then spend time going through it with them. Assure them that decisions are not being made without valid information.

Reading and then Responding

Reading behaviors through this matrix may help you increase healthy communication and minimize escalating emotional strife. High EQ leaders know how to keep others focused by understanding what is concerning them most and then responding appropriately.

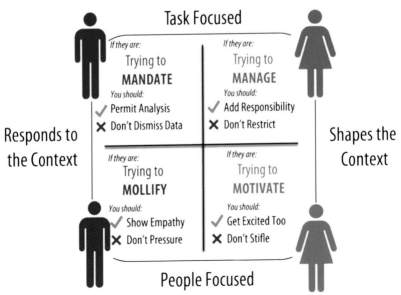

Task Focused

If they are:
Trying to
MANDATE
You should:
✓ Permit Analysis
✗ Don't Dismiss Data

If they are:
Trying to
MANAGE
You should:
✓ Add Responsibility
✗ Don't Restrict

Responds to the Context

Shapes the Context

If they are:
Trying to
MOLLIFY
You should:
✓ Show Empathy
✗ Don't Pressure

If they are:
Trying to
MOTIVATE
You should:
✓ Get Excited Too
✗ Don't Stifle

People Focused

No one leads with EQ perfectly, but there are those who do it better than others through intentionality mixed with humility.

And in reference to the opening reflections of an emotionally aware leader… Congratulations to Clark, the new VP of Sales! ■

//

SELF-REFLECTION EXERCISE

Mark the top 3 EQ traits that you need to work on. How will you improve each?

EQ Trait	How will you improve it?
☐ Accessibility	
☐ Active Listening	
☐ Attunement	
☐ Communication	
☐ Conflict	
☐ Developing Others	
☐ Empathy	
☐ Framing	
☐ Friendliness	
☐ Humor	
☐ Mood Management	
☐ Passion/Motivation	
☐ Problem Solving	
☐ Relationships/Connections	
☐ Self-Awareness	
☐ Self-Regulation	
☐ Social Skills	
☐ Stress Management	
☐ Teamwork	
☐ Thoughtful Questions	
☐ Use of Power	

It is during our darkest moments that we must focus to see the light.

Aristotle Onassis

CHAPTER FOUR

LEADERS BEHAVING BADLY

14 LEADERSHIP BEHAVIORS THAT CAUSE HARM
BY JAY R. DESKO, Ph.D.

Think of those you admire, those who had a positive influence on you and others. Now, think of someone who you did not respect, someone who had little positive influence and often had a negative impact on others. What was it about the person you did not respect that made him or her different from the hundreds of other people you have met? What sets him or her apart? In our years of reviewing other writers and research, as well as observing behaviors in our consulting with hundreds of leaders and organizations, we have come to realize that healthy leaders are not super-human, but they are different. And leaders who manifest bad behaviors are not all bad, but they can cause harm to themselves, others, and the health of their organization.

One of the fascinating observations about the Bible is that God does not sanitize His leaders behaving badly, reminding us that any leader can manifest healthy behavior at one time and unhealthy behavior the next. King Saul possessed great power but was crippled by his insecurity. King David was an exceptional leader but impulsively went after a married woman. King Solomon had extraordinary wisdom, but even he slipped into a string of foolish choices. Samson had super-human strength but failed to listen to his parents' counsel regarding dating partners. In the New Testament, John Mark was given a great opportunity to work with Paul but was freaked out by fear.

Now consider two more recent examples of leaders, Sarah and Jake. Sarah had held successful positions in two financial service businesses and a Christian non-profit. Her reputation was consistently positive, regardless of where she served. She was viewed as trustworthy and was also able to make hard decisions and deliver consistent results, all while caring about those around her. Don't misunderstand, not everyone thought highly of her. She was not super-human, but she consistently had a positive impact on most of those around her. This held true for over 45 years of leadership.

Jake had held a number of leadership roles in his lifetime. He had held eight positions in a variety of churches and Christian organizations. People were inspired by his public communication skills. In front of a group, he could sell snow to an Alaskan in the dead of winter! However, when he wasn't in front of a group speaking, he would hunker down in his office, use his secretary to keep people away from him, and avoid spending time with his colleagues. In each of his positions, he would start out strong but eventually either begin to lose credibility or end up in the midst of conflict by thinking he knew better than the other leaders around him. It was almost as if he was the Wizard of Oz. At first glance, Jake was powerful and significant. But when the curtain blew back, he was just a little man with a few tools and tricks that made him look greater than he was. It was all just an illusion. At least the wizard could acknowledge the trick when he was exposed. However, when Jake was exposed, he never acknowledged his short-comings. He blamed others and eventually would either quit and move on to another position or be asked to resign. He demonstrated a rather simple yet pathetic pattern: present a good show during interviews, impress people early on, hit a time of dissatisfaction, and then, move out. He too was certainly not super-human, but his bad behaviors resulted in serious negative side effects for himself and others.

Like all of us, Jake and Sarah are human with inherent talents and gifts as well as limitations and weaknesses. So, what behaviors differentiated Jake from Sarah? We have identified and explained the top fourteen bad behaviors that harm a leader's effectiveness and influence. As you continue reading, look for one or two with which you may personally relate to. This chapter will also offer steps to help you manage these behaviors if any are prevalent in your life.

14 Types of Leaders Behaving Badly

01 The Toxic Leader
If people can't get along with me, that's their problem!

02 The Conflict Avoiding Leader
Jesus was a peacemaker, and so am I.

03 The Proud Leader
I'm not arrogant. I'm just confident.

04 The Control Freak Leader
I cannot, not be in charge!

05 The Defensive Leader
You made this mistake, not me!

06 The Lukewarm Leader
I'm not unmotivated. I'm just content.

07 The Free Range Leader
I don't like boundaries. I need freedom!

08 The Narcissist Leader
I'm special, and I know it.

09 The Socially Clueless Leader
I'm not dysfunctional. I'm just not a people person.

10 The Distractible Leader
I have a really great idea, again!

11 The Non-Resilient Leader
When the going gets tough, run!

12 The Intentionally Deaf Leader
I can hear you. I just choose not to listen to you.

13 The NO Can Do Leader
I'm sorry, but the answer is NO.

14 The Silent Suffering Leader
If you only knew how I am really feeling!

1. THE TOXIC LEADER

If people can't get along with me, that's their problem!

Sue was the director of a non-profit social service agency who was despised by many. Even with all of her social service education, she had emerged as a nasty and unwelcome leader. Sue was known to yell at employees for not doing what she expected, ridicule team members in the middle of a meeting in front of their peers, and threaten to fire people when she got really angry. Employees and a few board members quietly referred to her as "the witch" and used words like "mean," "angry," "unpredictable," and "volatile" to describe their perceptions of her. While it took far too long for the board to intervene, she was eventually confronted and dismissed. To no surprise, she was nasty and aggressive on her way out the door.

Toxic leaders cause harm. They are like cancer cells in that they may start out normal or benign, but over time, they move from normal to dangerous and damaging behaviors. Toxic leaders manifest a number of "markers" including:
- Failing to reflect values of civility
- Deliberately misleading followers
- Using threat and intimidation to control others
- Setting people against one another
- Leaving people damaged and cynical
- Being unapproachable
- Creating undiscussables between them and the staff
- Causing good people to leave

Since such leaders may actually be producing short-term results and many people are afraid of them, whistle-blowers are often ignored or even dismissed. Sometimes it takes a catastrophic event like a lawsuit or major moral or criminal episode before the harm of a toxic leader is stopped. After the dust settles, the carnage of their bad behavior is self-evident.

2. THE CONFLICT AVOIDING LEADER
Jesus was a peacemaker, and so am I.

 If you were to look up a picture of a peacemaker, it could easily be Mike. As a Christian pastor, Mike took seriously the biblical instruction to live at peace with all people. This is a very noble goal in some circumstances. However, as a leader of a church, you sometimes have to make tough decisions, decisions that will result in someone not liking you. Mike's solution was to avoid conflict at all costs. One of his tactics was to agree with one person or group's ideas and then agree with another person or group even though the two views opposed each other! This would infuriate people who, in private conversations, would make disparaging remarks about Mike being duplicitous and lacking a backbone. In addition, he failed to hold poor performing staff accountable, he did not disagree with any board discussion, and he avoided confronting a church member who was acting inappropriately. In his pursuit of avoiding conflict, he ended up losing credibility and the respect of many around him.

Mike was manifesting what Edwin Friedman called "a failure of nerve." In *A Failure of Nerve: Leadership in the Age of the Quick Fix*, Friedman describes characteristics of someone like Mike:

A highly anxious risk-avoider, someone who is more concerned with good feelings than with progress, someone whose life revolves around the axis of consensus, a 'middler', someone who is so incapable of taking well-defined stands that his 'disability' seems to be genetic, someone who functions as if she had been filleted of her backbone, someone who treats conflict or anxiety *like mustard gas – one whiff, on goes the emotional gas mask, and he flits. Such leaders are nice if not charming.*

3. THE PROUD LEADER

I'm not arrogant. I'm just confident.

 Tim was the newly appointed general manager of a medium-sized business. Although he was young and had an untested track record in successful leadership, he did have nice academic credentials and plenty of confidence. However, even though he mesmerized many with his eloquent speaking abilities and spoke with great confidence, it did not take long before people saw the other side of him that moved beyond confidence into arrogance. He knew what was best, and he was going to make the changes he wanted regardless of what others thought. After all, he was very book smart! When members of his staff or leadership team pushed back, they paid the price of alienation and sometimes even termination. He was a proud leader and well on his way to destroying himself and the organization entrusted to him.

There is a big difference yet fine line between confidence and arrogance. Confidence generally grows from a proven long-term record of success. Arrogance grows from an over-inflated view of self and is centered in the heart of a person who is proud. In other words, confidence grows from evidence while arrogance grows from fallenness. Leaders such as Tim cannot see themselves as proud especially since those closest to them may not see it or would be too fearful of telling them. Such leaders are slow to ask for help and quick to blame others. They don't value their staff's skills or experience and therefore don't ask for input or build a collaborative work environment. God hates pride and explains that the proud person will generate conflict and ultimately experience humility and disgrace.

4. THE CONTROL FREAK LEADER
I cannot, not be in charge!

Alan was a gifted visionary. He had a passion to start a new church that would be a different kind of church. And it succeeded in a big way, at least for awhile. At first 30 people came, then 50, then 150, and eventually 450 people were attending. They went from using rental space to eventually owning a phenomenal 25-acre property with a worship center, office complex, and youth building. The staff expanded, the budget grew, and the impact was at an all time high when the small signs of something not right began to grow faster and faster. Alan was trying to control every element of the church including how the offices were decorated, what meetings the volunteers were required to attend, how the youth ministry was managed, and even how the trees were pruned! After almost 20 years, the exciting, vibrant ministry collapsed upon Alan, and he tried to control it, even to the very day when he was voted out of leadership.

Highly controlling behavior can result in or be the result of some of the other bad behaviors. For example, people who are narcissists, proud, or highly fearful can become control freaks even though it may be for different reasons. Some leaders believe they know better or that others will never do it as well as them. Other leaders are highly controlling because of their desire to guard their own position or reputation. Still others are very gifted leaders who possess critical thinking skills and keen insights. They can often see things others cannot. However, if they are too dedicated to being perfectionists, they may become a source of irritation by not trusting the skills and judgments of others. Regardless of the reasons, control freaks will likely cause harm to themselves by becoming overwhelmed (it's a lot of work trying to control everything!) and will drive away top talent.

5. THE DEFENSIVE LEADER
You made the mistake, not me!

 When confronted with a mistake or suggested improvement, Dave became like a Pit-Bull set after a poodle. He would attack "the enemy." Dave was the president of a small college. He was a very gifted leader being both entrepreneurial and charismatic in his influence. However, like many leaders, he had the bad behavior of becoming defensive when something would go wrong. One time, after receiving some tough criticism on a Leader 360 Feedback Evaluation, he became so angry that he confronted a number of employees and blamed them for the challenges he was facing. As his defensiveness grew, those around him became increasingly unwilling to tell him the truth. After all, they were the problem, not him! Eventually, Dave was encouraged to move on, which he did defending himself all the way to his next job.

It is common for people to respond with defensive routines when given feedback they may not believe or want to hear. Defensive routines often hinder the recipient from learning and may influence the giver to choose to withhold feedback. Some of the most common defensive routines include: blaming, attacking, denying, withdrawing, and spiritualizing. Being challenged or critiqued regarding such issues can create defensiveness in pastors, just like in anyone else. In his book, *Overcoming Organizational Defenses*, Dr. Chris Argyris states that defensive responses often grow out of a fear of embarrassment or threat. There are sometimes common, but perhaps unspoken, reasons for defensiveness including feeling under-appreciated, handling chronic health issues, dealing with the unlikelihood of being able to find another job, and experiencing anxiety from possibly having to move away from family and friends. If the underlying reasons are not acknowledged, Christian leaders can gloss over them by spiritualizing what is happening.

Spiritualization often occurs when a sound decision-making process is eliminated. It takes a variety of forms including inappropriately placing God's approval on a decision, confusing prayer with decision-making, misapplication of the Bible, and labeling others as unspiritual. Spiritualization artificially simplifies the issue and seldom leads to wise decisions. Ultimately, it abuses and trivializes God and His Word. Spiritualization often results in attacking others who disagree.

6. **THE LUKEWARM LEADER**

I'm not unmotivated. I'm just content.

 Chris has been in pastoral ministry for over 24 years and has served in his present church for the past seven years. Chris was a good dad, husband, and was well liked by many. However, it seemed each of the four churches he led over the years was flat when he arrived and flat when he left. Neither the churches nor Chris showed any signs of momentum. When Chris leaves his present church, it is likely the church will neither be much better or much worse. It will be nice and lukewarm, just like its leader.

While contentment can be a good trait when it comes to material possessions and other desires, it can also reflect low energy or worse, laziness, lack of innovation, and absence of passion. In some ways, lukewarm leaders manifest a failure to thrive. They don't push themselves very hard and they attract followers similar to themselves. Donors, potential employees, and volunteers seldom follow these leaders because they provide very few reasons to be followed.

7. THE FREE RANGE LEADER
I don't like boundaries. I need freedom!

In many ways, Jason was a really talented guy. He was outgoing, technically skilled and always looking for the next social party. However, he did not like people directing his path especially when their path was different than his. For Jason, the word "submission" was a very bad word. It made him cringe inside. Jason's supervisor would guide him, coach him and even threaten him. Being the social guy that he was, Jason never really fought back. Instead, he just didn't do what he was asked. He wanted freedom, and he wanted to be free range. He wanted to be given a salary and benefits but did not want any expectations placed upon him that he felt were confining. His unwillingness to listen to guidance and his desire for freedom ultimately caused him to step beyond the appropriate professional boundaries, resulting in his termination. Now he is truly free range!

Free range leaders don't like boundaries. Sometimes gifted free range leaders become successful entrepreneurs, business owners, and church planters. But even in these cases, if a free range leader does not have boundaries, he will fail. Failures may include sexual violations, financial mismanagement, misuse of employee time, or not fulfilling job responsibilities. The consequences of such an undisciplined and uncontrolled spirit can be catastrophic with terrible collateral damage to family, co-workers, and the organization.

8. THE NARCISSIST LEADER
I'm special, and I know it.

A number of people who worked with Steve found him to have some real talent, but when describing him, they often used terms such as "self-centered," "has a high view of himself," "entitled," and "likes to draw attention to himself." Even though he was a relatively young leader, he was known to use his assistant to screen his calls and email and spend an excessive amount of time outside of work (and sometimes inside) preparing for speaking and writing engagements. Steve's low self-awareness and high view of himself was a nasty combination which eventually led to his self-destruction.

Narcissists are people who have an extraordinarily high view of themselves and an exaggerated view of their uniqueness and strengths which results in extraordinary self-centeredness. Pride and narcissism are symbiotically connected and result in devastating outcomes for the leader and those around him. In an interesting study, narcissism was identified as one of the top two reasons of why intelligent people make dumb choices (Feinberg and Tarrant, *Why Smart People Do Dumb Things*).

Some of the common signs of narcissistic leaders include:
- Assuming their vision is correct
- Having a sense of entitlement
- Blaming others for failure
- Withholding information to accomplish their goals
- Depending upon rhetorical skills to cover problems
- Transferring focus from God to themselves

As noted in Chapter 1, "Narcissistic personalities . . . are frequently encountered in top management positions. Indeed, it is only to be expected that many narcissistic people, with their need for power, prestige, and glamour, eventually end up in leadership positions. Their sense of drama, their ability to manipulate others, and their knack for establishing quick, superficial relationships serve them well in organizational life" . . . but only for a season. (Manfred F. R. Kets De Vries, *Leaders, Fools, and Impostors*)

9. THE SOCIALLY CLUELESS LEADER

I'm not dysfunctional. I'm just not a people person.

 Mark is a classic example of a leader who repels people rather than attracts them. He was hired as the new director of a mid-sized non-profit organization. During his first year, significant conflict arose between Mark and most of the other staff and board members. While liked by some, an increasing number of people were experiencing Mark as short-tempered, autocratic, and relationally aloof. Some colleagues began to avoid any contact with Mark, resist his leadership, and talk among themselves about how much they hated working in this new environment. While his associates had their own deficits that contributed to this situation, Mark had developed an approach to leadership that was dissonant in its nature. He lacked self-awareness and did not wisely manage his relationships with those he served. When confronted with the perceptions of others, Mark was shocked and angry, justifying and viewing himself as a victim rather than the victimizer. Like most socially clueless leaders, Mark just didn't get it!

It is easy to assume that those who are good relaters are the people who are extroverts, gregarious, and always working the room. However, that would be a mistake. While some relaters do show these traits, there are many who are equally influential but more reserved and less comfortable up in front of the crowd. Whether you are an introvert or extrovert is not the key. Healthy leaders may not always be the smartest in the academic arena, but they are often the smartest in managing relationships with others.

Dr. Daniel Goleman is one of the most visible academic leaders in the field of Emotional Intelligence (EQ). He defines people who attract others as "resonant leaders" and those who repel others as "dissonant leaders." From our experience, people who are highly influential have a greater ability to attract others. The more a person is dissonant, the less likely they are to be able to influence others. Resonant leaders understand unspoken relational cues that others send and are more likely to use those cues in managing their behaviors and in seeking feedback from those around them. However, dissonant leaders have a pattern of behavior that includes at least some of the following:

- Missing social cues
- Verbal vomiting
- Absence of social capital
- Being socially awkward
- Lack of empathy and emotion
- Combative behaviors

Research has consistently shown that building strong relationships at work and at home is more about having the right ratio of interactions than it is about having no negative interactions. This ratio is ensuring you have five positive interactions for every negative. The socially clueless leader may count an interaction as positive, but to the other person, it was neutral at best. While most of us don't carry an interaction tracker in our pocket that technically monitors this, leaders would be wise to monitor it with intentional self-awareness.

10. THE DISTRACTIBLE LEADER

I have a really great idea, again!

Stan had some really good strengths. He was outgoing and creative and had high energy. His brain also moved at 15,000 RPM (if you don't know what that means – it's really fast!). He loved listening to podcasts, reading books, going to seminars, and trying new ideas, and a lot of them. Many of his employees started to refer to him as "Stan the idea man." Some of the ideas were good, but the volume of them, as well as the fact that some of the ideas seemed to conflict with other ideas he had proposed, made it challenging for the staff. There were times when one idea was not even successfully implemented before he was proposing the next idea. People became increasingly cynical and frustrated with Stan, not so much by the ideas but by the amount and lack of clear strategy or implementation. But since he was the boss, they endured it, at least for a while.

There are three phases of innovation: idea generation, evaluation, and implementation. Distractible leaders like Stan are often better at the generation phase but sometimes slip when it comes to either evaluation or implementation. The real challenge of this type of leader is their inability to focus. In his book, *Focus,* Daniel Goleman makes the research-based case of the connection between focus and excellence. People have limited capacity for processing an overabundance of information and distractions. Some researchers believe we actually only have the capacity for managing about four chunks of information at a time. Economist Herbert Simon said, "A wealth of information creates a poverty of attention." When you combine the uniqueness of people's personalities and brain functions with technology, an overabundance of information, and emotional distractions, it is amazing that anyone can focus! But we have seen firsthand that leaders can and do learn to be disciplined and focused, and subsequently experience the rewards.

11. THE NON-RESILIENT LEADER
When the going gets tough, run!

 Tom was such a nice guy. He was married, had three children, and was a vice president in a mid-sized company. Many admired Tom for his gifted leadership and commitment to family. But he had one crack in his armor. He was easily defeated. When Tom's wife was diagnosed with cancer and he experienced pressure from a major project at work, he felt so overwhelmed that he began looking for escape routes. He searched the internet for new jobs (one with less stress) and spent time at the bar to dampen the pain of his wife's illness and treatments. Most people can understand how overwhelmed Tom must have felt. Many people have experienced suffering and disappointment and even a number of them at the same time. The difference is that Tom struggled with a lack of resiliency. In other words, he did not have the ability to bounce back from difficulty. His first and only coping strategy was to escape it, not endure it.

One of the differentiating disciplines of successful leaders is that they consistently manifest a resolve to show grit and not easily quit. Grit is a term being used by psychologist Angela Lee Duckworth of The University of Pennsylvania and others to creatively describe a character trait commonly known as self-discipline. Such discipline seems to have been more prevalent among the WWII and older generations and appears less with each new generation. Today, we increasingly see people sign up but not show up, start but not finish, and promise but not deliver. This is true in education (starting but not finishing college), volunteerism (signing up but not following through), employment (making a commitment but then leaving for another opportunity), health care (beginning a diet and exercise routine but bailing after a few months), and marriage (saying "I do" but living like "I do, for now"). Grit can often become the determining factor of those who finish well and those who do not.

12. THE INTENTIONALLY DEAF LEADER
I can hear you. I just choose not to listen to you.

 Nancy was a talented leader who was well liked and successful. Sometimes she would seek advice and listen. Other times however, she would either not see the need to seek input on an important decision or would ask for advice but not listen to it. On a few occasions, she ignored some very important and wise counsel and the consequences were devastating. For example, her friends advised her to not marry the guy she was dating, but she went ahead with it anyway. After a lot of lawyer's fees, tears, and loss of money, she acknowledged she should have listened. On another occasion, a supervisor advised her to start spending more time with her colleagues in order to build trust. However, she didn't listen and was deeply hurt and angered when some of them began talking about her in unflattering ways. Nancy was experiencing the side-effects of the intentionally deaf leader.

Listening is hard work even for the most disciplined. Our personalities, the speed at which our brains process information, and the number of distractions that cause interference all contribute to the challenge. However, that is not an excuse for failing to listen, especially when it relates to important relationships and serious decisions. Few people acknowledge they are intentionally not listening, but rather, they rationalize their dismissal of information as being justified. In the end, the intentionally deaf leader will pay the price by trying to correct the bad decisions that could have been prevented more easily in the first place.

In their exceptional book, *Mistakes Were Made (But Not by Me)*, social psychologists Carol Tavris and Elliot Aronson explain that when faced with perceptions or data different from our own, we have a strong propensity to dismiss, discredit, or distort both the perceptions and those who hold to them. They note, "Most people, when directly confronted by evidence that they are wrong, do not change their point of view or course of action, but justify it even more tenaciously. Even irrefutable evidence is rarely enough to pierce the mental armor of self-justification."

13. THE NO CAN DO LEADER
I'm sorry, but the answer is NO.

Hank was a department manager of a non-profit organization. He had been with the organization for over 20 years in a number of different roles. Although he was friendly, creative, and possessed good critical thinking skills, he had one particularly annoying habit – leading with NO. When people would ask him for project assistance, he would share why it cannot be done. When new ideas were floated, he would often note why they may not work. When asked why a project was not completed, he always had a reason or an excuse depending upon who he was talking with. In spite of being well liked, Hank experienced the common consequences of the NO can do leader. He lost his credibility and people bypassed him to get to a YES!

Hank is not alone. There are many "NO can do leaders." Whether it was from their upbringing, personal insecurity, issues of control, the nature of their unique personality wiring, or some combination, the outcome is unfortunate. They quench the creative thinking of others, train others to also lead with NO, create a culture of excuse-making, and cause others to work around them. We have never seen a leader experience long-term success or have a significant impact by leading with NO. This is not to say that NO is never a legitimate answer. On the contrary, wise leaders must know when to say NO, but it is the exception, seldom the rule. Effective leaders do not make excuses, they make results. As a rule, they do not lead with NO; instead they lead with YES!

14. THE SILENT SUFFERING LEADER

If you only knew how I am really feeling!

 When Sue joined the board of the local non-profit rescue mission, she was a highly esteemed business leader and active in her local church. She was friendly, hard-working, and family oriented, and she added great value to the board and mission with her leadership experience and vision. Sue often spoke in positive ways about her children and her husband, telling stories about vacations and weekend activities. They appeared to be a picture of a perfect family – one others admired and aspired to be like.

Therefore, Sue's announcement came as a major shock when she told the board chair that she was stepping down from her role as a board member because she was leaving her husband. Her friends and colleagues couldn't believe it. Confused would be an understatement. Even her husband didn't know how much she was struggling inside. Over the next few weeks, Sue shared with a few close friends that she was lonely, no longer loved her husband, and needed "out." This had been building for a few years, but she had never told anyone, not even her closest friends. Later on, it was discovered that she had been romantically involved with another man. Sue is just one example of a leader who was struggling in her private world but chose not to share her struggles with anyone else who could have helped her.

Silent suffering is not unique to Sue. Many people fear disclosing what they are struggling with on the inside. These struggles include dealing with pornography, substance addiction, infidelity, job discontentment, financial problems, difficulty with a child, or mental or emotional health issues. Those suffering fear sharing these struggles because they are embarrassing and can result in a damaged career, loss of friendships, or being accused of sharing too much about their personal life (emotional vomiting!). The higher up a person is in positions of leadership and influence, the harder it can be for the silent sufferer to invite others into his or her private world. While the fears and risks of disclosure are real, there are also consequences to withholding information that will impact this person's life and also impact the organization and those with whom they serve. After all, by not disclosing her struggle to a close friend or counselor, Silent Suffering Sue ended up bruising her reputation as well as her family and the rescue mission. Those around her felt violated by this unfortunate surprise, and she became more embarrassed and isolated by the awkwardness that resulted. When it comes to silent suffering of this kind, it is fair to say everyone loses.

WHAT'S A LEADER BEHAVING BADLY TO DO?

If you are like most leaders, you can uncomfortably resonate with at least one or two of the bad behaviors. Just because you are a leader behaving badly, that does not mean you are a bad leader. You can change by addressing these behaviors. It would take a very thick book to begin to describe what is needed to better manage and grow out of each behavior. However, here are some common steps that we have seen work successfully.

1. Face reality

One of the first and most difficult steps for a leader who is behaving badly is to face reality. This means courageously examining yourself and acknowledging your shortcomings and their effects on those around you. You may need to acknowledge these faults to your team and express a desire to change. You may also need to ask forgiveness and pursue reconciliation in some relationships.

2. Humble yourself and be teachable

The Bible charges us to clothe ourselves with humility (1 Peter 5:5). Yet, our natural bent is in the direction of arrogance and entitlement. One of the true signs of spiritual transformation is how we submit to those around us, which is not a popular concept in an age of growing cynicism with authority. Such submission requires humility. Signs of humility include listening, flexibility, sacrificing our own desires and will, and trusting the wisdom of others. Do you have a "truth teller" in your life who tells you the truth no matter if you are going to like it or not?

3. Be hopeful

Let's be realistic, no human leader is perfect or flawless. While this is stating the obvious, we often forget it and start to believe that other leaders really have it all together. While some leaders may have learned to manage their bad behaviors more effectively than others, most leaders will struggle with one or more of them. Any honest and self-aware leader will tell you just that. While we are all a bit broken in how we think and function, those who embrace the wisdom of the Bible can hold onto the hope that God is both forgiving and redemptive. Remember, Jesus came to provide forgiveness for the fallen, healing for the hurting, and hope for the hopeless.

Yes, my soul, find rest in God; my hope comes from him.
– Psalm 62:5
…but those who **hope** in the LORD will renew their strength. They will soar on wings like eagles; they will run and not grow weary, they will walk and not grow faint. – Isaiah 40:31

4. Reframe your thinking

How you think about your life and circumstances has a powerful effect on you and those around you. Highly anxious leaders can easily produce highly anxious families, workers, and organizations. Highly influential leaders also experience the pains and disappointments common in life. What sets them apart is not that they never think about their problems in an unhealthy way, but rather it is how effective they are at catching the thoughts early. They put off old and unhealthy thoughts, and put on new accurate thoughts. The Bible calls this renewing our minds by putting off our old self and being made new in the attitude of our minds (Romans 12:1-2, Ephesians 4:22-23, Philippians 4:8).

5. Seek feedback

We highly recommend that leaders who want to grow arrange an externally facilitated Leader 360 Feedback Process, just like in Chapter 3 where we recommend this for leaders who want to develop their EQ. A 360 feedback process includes gathering anonymous perspectives of how others see you as a leader. These perspectives include your own view of yourself and also the views of your supervisor(s), your peers, and those who report to you. Such feedback is one of the most accurate ways to identify strengths, bad behaviors, and possible blind spots. We cannot grow without feedback from others.

6. Manage your defensiveness

It is common for people to respond with defensive routines when given feedback they may not believe or want to hear. Defensive routines often hinder the recipient from learning and may influence the giver to choose to withhold feedback. As stated earlier, some of the most common defensive routines include blaming, attacking, denying, withdrawing, and spiritualizing. While such internal responses are common at first, a wise leader takes hold of them and manages them rather than letting the defensiveness manage him/her. Managing your defensiveness will help to create a safe environment for both you and those you lead.

7. Get a coach or mentor
Coaching from an experienced third party can help you become more open and flexible. Let's face it; feedback can be scary and threatening to even the most secure leader. A coach can help you make sense of what you are experiencing and what others are seeing in you. In addition, they can guide you through change and provide accountability and encouragement.

CONCLUSION
Remember Jake and Sarah from the introduction? Where you able to identify which behaviors differentiated Jake from Sarah? Jake exhibited characteristics of #3 The Proud Leader, #5 The Defensive Leader, #7 The Free Range Leader, and #8 The Narcissist Leader. His behaviors made it impossible for him to achieve long-term success in any leadership position and caused each organization under him to fail in reaching its fullest potential.

Sarah's ability to make tough decisions could have easily grown into #4 The Control Freak Leader, and her positive reputation could have developed into #3 The Proud Leader. However, the difference came because she was able to humble herself, seek the feedback of those around her, and respond with a willingness to learn. We genuinely desire that you are able to identify any hints of these behaviors in your own life and that you can work on eradicating them out of your life so you and your organization can achieve optimal health. ■

IN MATTERS OF STYLE,
SWIM WITH THE CURRENT.

IN MATTERS OF PRINCIPLE,
STAND LIKE A ROCK.

THOMAS JEFFERSON

SELF-REFLECTION EXERCISE

Mark the top 2 to 3 behaviors you have seen in your own life:

Steps to change this behavior:

1. The Toxic Leader
If people can't get along with me, that's their problem!

2. The Conflict Avoiding Leader
Jesus was a peacemaker, and so am I.

3. The Proud Leader
I'm not arrogant. I'm just confident.

4. The Control Freak Leader
I cannot, not be in charge!

5. The Defensive Leader
You made this mistake, not me!

6. The Lukewarm Leader
I'm not unmotivated. I'm just content.

7. The Free Range Leader
I don't like boundaries. I need freedom!

8. The Narcissist Leader
I'm special, and I know it.

9. The Socially Clueless Leader
I'm not dysfunctional. I'm just not a people person.

10. The Distractible Leader
I have a really great idea, again!

11. The Non-Resilient Leader
When the going gets tough, run!

12. The Intentionally Deaf Leader
I can hear you. I just choose not to listen to you.

13. The NO Can Do Leader
I'm sorry, but the answer is NO.

14. The Silent Suffering Leader
If you only knew how I am really feeling!

I've learned that
people will forget
what you said,
people will forget
what you did, but
people will never
forget how you
made them feel.
Maya Angelou

CHAPTER FIVE

THEIR NEEDS, YOUR NEEDS

BEING AN EFFECTIVE TEAM LEADER AND TEAM MEMBER
BY JAY R. DESKO, Ph.D.

Like city smog, toxic air can settle into the ethos of a team. It happens subtly, but before you know it, the morale is waning and the performance of the team is suffering. Seldom is it intentional, but ignoring a few simple principles can turn a high energy, high performing team environment into one where you hear more sighs than laughter and spend more time solving problems than celebrating progress.

Conversely, team leaders and team members can keep the fresh air of energy and excitement flowing freely by following these ten tried-and-true tactics for building team effectiveness. Both leaders and members play a key role in maintaining the health of the team. Use the following chapter as a mini-audit to see if you are doing your part well. Your team can benefit greatly by using this chapter as a discussion starter. Teams that get this right will experience the win-win effect since team leaders and team members share a symbiotic relationship. Teams, just like people in general, are best able to meet the needs of others when their needs have been met!

IF YOU ARE A TEAM MEMBER,
HERE IS WHAT YOUR LEADER NEEDS FROM YOU:

1. PRACTICE THE "NO SURPRISE RULE"

Sometimes surprises are fun, like a surprise party or gift. However, when it comes to your supervisor, he or she will not appreciate being surprised by learning, either second hand or after the fact, of problems, changes, or other things related to you and your department. Unwanted surprises can cause a leader to be embarrassed, and embarrassment often results in defensiveness and negative reactions. Examples of surprises include:

- A personal problem
- An emerging conflict
- A change that may be controversial

Practice the "no surprise rule" by keeping your supervisor informed, especially with any item that can result in him or her being embarrassed or caught off guard.

2. SHOW INITIATIVE

Team leaders love it when they see team members showing initiative and working hard. One way to do this is to identify and solve problems which will make the team look great and will advance the mission of the organization. Another way is to do more than is expected. In other words, exceed expectations; don't just try to meet them. Lastly, show relational initiative. Relationships require initiative from both parties; it is important that you take responsibility to pursue both your boss and peers. Good relational connection increases trust and relational capital which you will very likely need at some point in the near future. Sometimes, team members are intimidated by those in higher positions. Don't allow insecurity to hinder you. Take responsibility and pursue!

Pursue your supervisor and your team members:
- Ask them to lunch.
- Stop into their office regularly for a quick hello.
- Inquire as to how they and their family are doing.
- Seek input from them in order to learn and grow.

3. LEARN THEIR STYLE, VALUES, AND TRIGGERS
For any good relationship to survive in the long term, you have to know what makes people tick. This includes your supervisor. Take the time to learn his or her work style. For example, does he manifest high work energy or low work energy? What are her values? For example, does she value . . . timeliness? relationships? speed? quality? And, what triggers him? For example . . . being late? failing to follow through? sloppy dress? grammatical mistakes? By taking responsibility for knowing the leadership style, values, and triggers of your team leader, you will be able to adapt and build greater synergy and credibility.

4. LEAD WITH YES
"I don't have time.""Yes, but.""No." These are three responses from team members that can bring steam to a leader's head! It frustrates them and any member of the team who is a high performer. As leadership coaches, we often find ourselves advising team members to lead with "yes" rather than "no" or other deflecting excuses that lead to inaction or indecision. In one case, we provided feedback to a client that he was

being viewed as the "yes, but" staff member, and he was losing the credibility of the leaders and team members around him because of it. He took this to heart and began to change his behavior by focusing on more proactive and positive responses to those around him, in others words, leading with "yes." Within a few months, his supervisor shared that the transformation was amazing! Of course, we would never recommend leading with yes for inappropriate or unethical requests. That would not be smart!

5. LET YOUR LOYALTY SHOW

If you expect loyalty, show loyalty. Whereas water flows downwards, the natural flow of blame is often upwards! However, this seldom leads to team health or effective team performance. Showing loyalty does not mean that you should not shoot straight with those above you. On the contrary, it means if you have a concern or grievance, you need to be courageous enough to share it with your supervisor in an honest yet respectful manor. This can be a bit scary since you may be sharing something that he does not want to hear, especially since he holds your job in his hands.

However, leaders need both feedback and confidence so they can trust you. When a leader feels he or she cannot trust a team member, the trust and relational chemistry will erode the team's effectiveness and satisfaction. Face to face and honest sharing can demonstrate loyalty, but gossiping about them with others or going around them to their supervisor can feel like a breach of loyalty. However, it is not appropriate to allow loyalty to the leader to supersede loyalty to the well-being of the organization. You must balance loyalty to the leader with loyalty to the mission and health of the organization. This is not always easy to do, but the effort is well worth it.

1. PROVIDE CLEAR EXPECTATIONS

Imagine stepping onto a soccer field and scoring a goal only to have the referee blow the whistle and say it didn't count because he actually meant for you to play football, even though he never told you this! Sounds bizarre, but one of the most common complaints we hear from team members in a variety of organizations is, "I don't really know what's expected of me." While job descriptions serve a meaningful purpose in helping someone understand an overview of his or her position, leaders must be clear regarding what they want, what level of quality they expect, and when they want it by. Expectations should be realistic, specific, clear, and agreed upon.

2. GIVE REGULAR FEEDBACK

Quality feedback is direct, specific, and non-punishing. It is connected to clear expectations. It is hard to give good feedback to someone who doesn't know what is expected of them. Some experts believe that 80% of performance problems can be resolved by a leader providing clear expectations and feedback to a team member. There is no excuse for a team leader who does not give regular feedback for both excellent performance as well as problems. Giving quality feedback costs nothing other than a little time and courage!

Quality feedback:
- May be used for affirmation, teaching, or correcting
- Should not surprise the recipient in a negative way
- Should be ongoing and two-way
- Should be based upon clear expectations

3. LEAD BY EXAMPLE

As a leader, it is your job to model the behaviors you want to see in others.

- If you want hard work, model it.
- If you want openness to feedback, practice it yourself.
- If you want collaboration, be collaborative.
- If you want timely delivery on projects, perform the same way yourself.
- If you want relationships, pursue them.

You are setting the tone and creating the team DNA as much by what you do as by what you say. Set the example by modeling the performance, relational style, and work energy you want to see in others.

4. SPEND TIME WITH THEM

One of the greatest resources for a team member is you, the team leader. Some team leaders keep their distance from team members, seldom spending regular time connecting. This social distance often results in diminishing trust, lower relational capital, less opportunities to influence team members, and fewer opportunities for them to give feedback to you. A number of years ago, researcher John Kotter did a study on how effective leaders spent their time. He discovered they spend upwards of 90% of their time in relational connection and communication with their staff, both formal and informal. Spend time with the members of your team!

Ideas of how to spend more time with your team include:
- Brief office visits
- Formal meetings
- Lunch together

5. RECOGNIZE EFFORT AND EXCELLENCE

I remember an office worker who had trouble doing her work with quality. Her manager's solution was to take important projects and give them to a more competent staff member. Over a period of a year or two, she was rewarded with less and less work, even though she was one of the highest paid! She had less and less responsibility and pressure. And the more competent worker had more and more. Who was rewarded? The incompetent worker! This is far more common than you might expect. Leaders must focus on recognizing and rewarding excellence, not incompetence. Here are three particular and practical ways to show recognition for effort and excellent performance:

Praise: Let them and others know how well they are doing. This can be done directly to the person, in a team meeting so others can see and hear it, in a handwritten thank you note, in an email, or even in a newsletter. In one case, I wanted to praise the excellent service provided by three employees of an organization, so I wrote an email to the president praising them and copied them on it. He felt affirmed that his team did so well, and they felt great having the president hear about their hard work!

Reward: Praise is nice, but I never met a person who did not appreciate a Starbucks gift card! Some practical and easy to deliver rewards include a bonus, free lunch for the team or privately with the team leader, a gift card, a weekend away certificate, time off, or even a team party. Be creative. It's not only the dollar value of the reward, it is also the appreciation it communicates.

Opportunity: Motivated team members often want new opportunities to learn, grow, and advance. This is true for most people who desire to keep growing and advancing and is especially true for millennials. Examples of new opportunities may include new projects, new positions, workshops and seminars, and paying for further education.

The flow of needs goes both ways in an organization. The leader's needs must be met by his team in order to lead well, and the team members' needs must be met by the leader in order to perform well. Often, if one person's needs are not being met, he can throw off everyone around him and begin to stifle the air. We hope the five key needs we have identified for each party will help your team learn the art of managing up and managing down and provide clearer, more breathable air.

KEY NEEDS SUMMARY

If you are a team member...

1. Practice the "no surprise rule"

2. Show initiative

3. Learn your leader's style, values, and triggers

4. Lead with yes

5. Let your loyalty show

If you are a team leader...

1. Provide clear expectations

2. Give regular feedback

3. Lead by example

4. Spend time with your team

5. Recognize effort and excellence

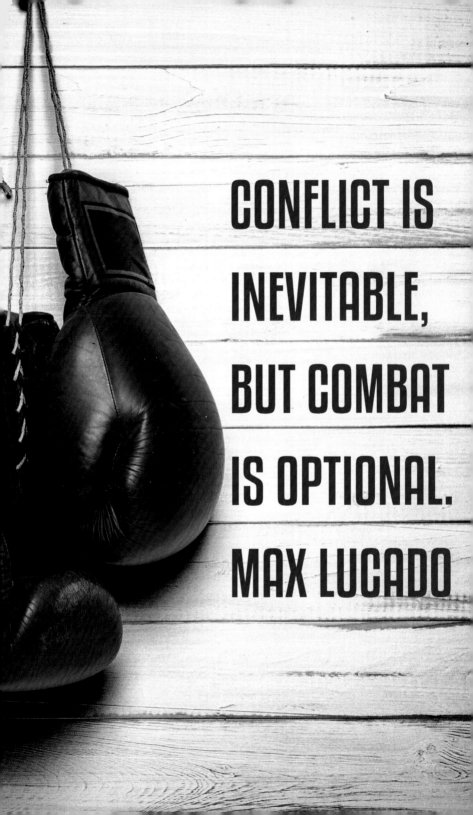

CONFLICT IS INEVITABLE, BUT COMBAT IS OPTIONAL. MAX LUCADO

CHAPTER SIX

THE HIGH COST OF CONFLICT

BY DAVID A. MARKS, D.Min.

Unresolved conflict in the workplace is expensive on many fronts. The decrease of productivity, having low morale, the forming of unhealthy alliances, the resulting turnover rate, and the ever-increasing danger of violence have spawned numerous workplace policies, procedures, and training seminars. The concept of a disgruntled employee, volunteer, or customer "going postal" is on the mind of leaders everywhere.

However, what you will not hear in this chapter is that conflict is wrong or unnecessary; it is actually quite the opposite. Conflict can be a critically important component in the formation of high-functioning teams. Diversity of viewpoints, experiences, personalities, and skillsets can make an environment ripe for conflict, but this diversity is also the engine that pushes organizations up and forward. The key is knowing how to allow the right amount and the right kind of conflict into the system without letting it escalate into a damaging dispute. To do this, we must understand the different root causes of conflict.

7 ROOT CAUSES OF CONFLICT
1. WE WANT SOMETHING WE CAN'T HAVE
Human history records horrendous conflicts that escalated to battles and wars that devastated entire regions of the world until one dominant ideology prevailed over another. The Bible addresses this very point when James, one of the disciples of Jesus, wrote, *"What causes fights and quarrels among you? Don't they come from your desires that battle within you? You desire but do not have, so you kill. You covet but you cannot get what you want, so you quarrel and fight"* (James 4:1-2). The bottom-line is if we allow our natural selfish tendencies to be the driving force in our life, we will get ticked-off whenever we don't get what we want, and then we will do whatever has to be done to get it. Even if nine out of ten people on a team have learned to manage these selfish impulses, there will still be problems because of the one.

2. PERSONAL VALUES ARE CHALLENGED
The way an individual views integrity will inevitably shape his or her personal code of ethical behavior. However, within every organization, there are lines in place that define its ethos and culture. The norms of the workplace and right and wrong are determined by what is expected; a form of Group Think takes hold. Conflict arises when these expectations clash against personal values. This clash can be intensified when religious teachings and cultural values based on ethnicity and nationality are added to the mix. For some, the conflict surrounds the pace and priority of the work they do, in which case the amount of hours someone is in the building may

matter more than if they "fudge the numbers" a bit or put a twist on the truth to maintain the allusion that "all is well." When one's personal integrity clashes with the expected outcomes from the manager or the larger group, expect conflict to arise. When my son was interviewing for a job, the interviewer was testing for this very dynamic. My son was asked about certain scenarios in which he would be willing to allow the company's welfare to determine his values. He replied, "Of this one thing you can be sure, I will never lie for you, but I will never lie to you." He got the job!

3. ROLE AMBIGUITY

Titles and pay grades can only prevent some role confusion. Circumstances often create opportunities for others to exercise their talents in someone else's territory, and thus the classic power struggle is born. (Of course, conflict can also happen if someone feels they are stuck doing someone else's responsibility.) The jealousy and intimidation that come from overlapping into someone else's territory can easily spark conflict. Ambiguity occurs more frequently within environments where there is more fluidity and less rigidity about titles. The absence of hierarchical structure can have large upsides when creating collaborative teams or doing joint projects, but beware if some good-spirited competition starts to turn towards conflict. Some members can start to secretly sabotage the work of others. To reduce role ambiguity, some work groups actually use a Team Charter to crystallize various roles, responsibilities, and expectations. This allows the team to stay focused on the stated objectives.

4. ASSET ALLOCATION

I once worked in a church setting where the policy on the use of equipment and facilities was on a first-come, first-served basis. In theory, it was a good policy. It rewarded those who were disciplined enough to plan ahead. The Youth Pastor was such a clever person; he booked the use of the church's gym every Saturday night a year in advance. He reserved the use of the church's two new vans every weekend. He planned his budget to front load the most expensive things early in the fiscal year before the budget got lean towards the end of the year. He was a genius! Right? Since he had all those things reserved, he had control of those assets. If you wanted to use them, you had to go seek his permission. Well, most weeks, the vans sat parked, and the gym was empty. BUT the policy was being kept perfectly. Conflict ensued! Good planning involves having a holistic view of the assets to be shared and making sure everyone is able to access the resources they need to accomplish their part of the task. A shared calendar can go a long way to reducing this type of conflict.

5. WORK STYLES

It is fascinating to observe how different people learn, work, think, and express themselves. After experiencing a few personality charged conflicts in your organization, you might be tempted to think that if we could just group people of similar styles, we would have a workplace panacea. Wrong. We need the variety of styles to balance out the limitations inherent of any one style, not to mention the monotony of working with people just like ourselves!

Understanding these differences and actually appreciating this diversity goes a long way to keeping conflict from erupting. I have observed effective leaders fail in many different areas on the work style spectrum. The problem occurs when work styles clash rather than complement. For instance, some people need the structure of strict deadlines while others love the thrill of getting things done at the last minute. There is a plethora of books, articles, and instruments to expand your learning on this subject. The Center also offers specific testing for work styles and team chemistry based on self-reporting and input from others. The following chart defines four of the different work styles that team members may experience.

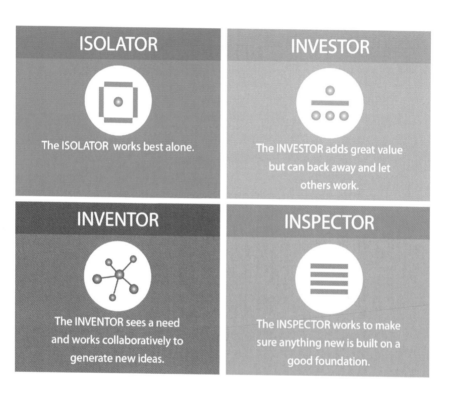

ISOLATOR
The ISOLATOR works best alone.

INVESTOR
The INVESTOR adds great value but can back away and let others work.

INVENTOR
The INVENTOR sees a need and works collaboratively to generate new ideas.

INSPECTOR
The INSPECTOR works to make sure anything new is built on a good foundation.

6. PERCEPTIONS

My wife is far-sighted and I am near-sighted. Because we each have a different strength with a corresponding weakness, we make a pretty good team. Without our glasses, we perceive the world differently. She can read road signs in the distance, but I can read menus. She keeps me from missing my exit, and I can tell her to order the chicken cacciatore. But when we both think we are absolutely right and the other person is totally wrong, there will be the inevitable conflict. What is at the core of the problem? Perceptions. Perceptions, as discussed in Chapter 2, are simply cognitive pictures that are stored in the brain. They develop as a result of a complex combination of factors including concrete experiences, cultural beliefs, and social influences. They are often treated as "the truth" from those who hold them, even if the perception is inaccurate, therefore making them very powerful. They can be changed through honest dialogue and changed behaviors.

When tensions are rising, increase communication by documenting why you have the perceptions you do and by actively listening to the viewpoints of others. Most of us have the tendency to try and connect the dots and make early conclusions in order to validate our own assumptions or perceptions. Therefore, the more "dots" of communication there are, the more likely you will be to arrive at an accurate conclusion or course of action.

Try using the following perceptual positioning exercise to help you test the validity of your perceptions. Attached to those perceptions are normally strong emotions. Ultimately, it is best if the facts govern the emotional aspects when it comes time to find solutions. But if others feel they have not been heard or their position is not fairly represented, it will be a challenge for them to let go of their emotions long enough to reveal the real nature of the problem to be solved.

Running the Bases of Perceptual Positioning

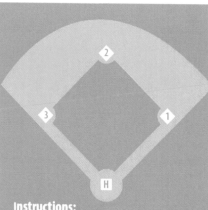

The best communicators have developed the skill to perceptually reposition themselves to see a situation from multiple viewpoints resulting in better critical thinking, problem solving, and resolution.

FIRST BASE: Your View
Articulate accurately how you see a situation. Provide rationale for your opinion that is NOT emotionally charged or skewed by personal bias.

SECOND BASE: Their View
Put yourself in the "other guy's shoes". Without sarcasm, honestly try to express the logic, motive, and goals of those who oppose or disagree with you.

THIRD BASE: Observer View
Like a jury, objectively weigh the merits of each of the positions and make a decision about what seems like the best/wisest scenario or conclusion for the organization.

HOME PLATE: Stakeholder View
Did the leaders act maturely and in my best interest? Or did their egos get in the way of making a good decision?

Instructions:
Put four pieces of paper on the ground and literally move from base to base recording your thoughts, ideas, and conclusions. Changing physical positions can help change perceptions. In conflict resolution, a moderator can help the conflicting parties to walk through this process until they come to an amiable and wise agreement.

At each base, ask the following questions:
What do they WANT?
What do they NEED?
What are their CONCERNS?
What are their CONSTRAINTS?
What are their PRESSURES?

7. CONFLICTING DEFINITIONS OF SUCCESS OR THE "WIN"

I have a friend who is a printer, and I remember seeing this sign in his front office.

WE OFFER 3 KINDS OF SERVICES
GOOD – CHEAP – FAST
BUT YOU CAN ONLY PICK TWO
GOOD & CHEAP WON'T BE FAST
FAST & GOOD WON'T BE CHEAP
CHEAP & FAST WON'T BE GOOD

The sign is clever and correct. The customer is forced to pick two and forfeit the third. Likewise, leaders can inadvertently communicate conflicting goals which in turn causes conflict. For instance, one staff member might be pushing his team to meet deadlines because conveying speed is the most important goal, while another staff person might be telling his team that excellence is the top priority, and the business manager may be tightening the purse strings to keep things within the budget. The result is confusion and conflict.

RESOLVING CONFLICT

Not surprisingly, organizations, like friendships, can grow stronger as a result of conflict being resolved appropriately. When respect is gained, trust can grow. Consider adopting this four stage approach to conflict management.

STAGE 1: PREPARING FOR RESOLUTION

Conduct a self-examination. I once had a doctor tell me to wake up every morning, take a good look in the mirror, and if I see *three* of anything, to give him a call ☺. If you have been in leadership long enough, you can easily go back and remember the conflicts you have experienced. Some were painful and have left scars that you can still see when you look inside. The good news is that you learned something. You now know what NOT to do as well as valuable principles to use when conflict happens the next time. It is good to remember that the standard is not perfection but peaceableness. If it is not egregious, dangerous, or unethical, you can choose to let some things go. You can choose not to be offended. Responding impulsively when someone hits a nerve in us emotionally can ratchet up conflict quickly. Try practicing the Principle of First Response.

Principle of First Response

"A gentle answer turns away wrath, but a harsh word stirs up anger." – Proverbs 15:1

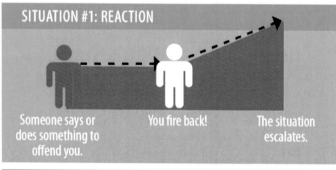

"Live in harmony with one another...Do not be conceited. Do not repay anyone evil for evil. Be careful to do what is right in the eyes of everyone. If it is possible, as far as it depends on you, live at peace with everyone." –Romans 12:16-18

Reflect on these questions:
- What are my hot buttons?
- Am I being too sensitive?
- What defensive routines show up first when I sense a conflict coming?
- What attitudes are warning signs that I am beginning to escalate the conflict?
- What is the best case scenario for how this conflict ends?

Install smoke detectors. Good leaders can smell smoke before there is a fire. Early intervention has saved many from the lingering negative effects of when conflict gets out of control. There is a tendency for people to ignore the first signs of conflict hoping it will get smoothed over quickly. Other managers jump in too early and too hard which drives the problem below the surface to smolder. Usually, this latent conflict shows up insidiously in unpredictable environments down the road. However, it can be difficult for managers to differentiate between healthy banter and a fuse being lit that will go KA-BOOM in a couple of hours, days, weeks, or months. It is easier to maintain trust and morale than it is to try and rebuild it.

Confrontation is a precious gift. When it is withheld, teams deteriorate, performances fail, families break apart, and companies go bankrupt. The lack of appropriate, effective confrontation is fatal to communities, and it can be lethal to individual men and women.
– Jon Ortberg

I saw this type of intervention beautifully managed by a flight attendant on a flight from Nashville to Philadelphia. Sitting five rows in front of me were two people exchanging words with some heat in them. It was a man and a woman, but they were not married. I could feel the tension rising quickly, and I was pretty sure she could take him. I was just waiting for the first swing when down the aisle comes a tiny flight attendant who might have weighed 90 pounds (if she was carrying a brick or two). Without hesitation, she stood between them, and with a deep, loud bass voice said, "This ends here, and it ends now! Do I make myself clear?" In typical Nashville style, they both sheepishly said "yes ma'am" and sat down. Our whole section cheered and they sat in their seats without a peep for the rest of the flight. Problem solved!

Try talking it out in private. Airing grievances in public is a mistake to be avoided. Nobody likes to be embarrassed in front of peers or made an example of in public. You are showing respect to the person when you suggest a neutral private setting. However, if you need to emphasize your authority over a direct report, a manager's office may be appropriate. Some experts suggest arranging the furniture so that there are no physical objects like tables between you. Eye-to-eye contact with no more than an arm's length between the two parties dramatically increases the likelihood of positive body language that will create an environment of openness rather than hostility.

Usually, destructive conflict is about feelings not facts. Therefore, practice using "I" statements instead of "you" statements that put others on the defensive because they feel like they are being attacked. Instead of saying, "You make me so mad," rephrase it like, "I feel really frustrated when you ____." Take responsibility for your emotions and reactions. Let the other party do the same. You might be surprised to find that when you are sharing how you feel in certain circumstances, the real emotion is fear not anger. If an amiable agreement to solve the conflict cannot be found in private, it's time to agree to get others involved. Hire a skilled facilitator if necessary.

Come prepared to offer and hear alternative proactive solutions. Being prepared for a resolution means you acknowledge you will likely have to sacrifice something to get to a win-win. Conflict is not always about negotiation. Frequently, there is an absolute right way, an absolute wrong way, or the boss' way. However, most conflict has an element of give-n-take in order to move toward pro̲covery. In re̲covery, the parties must do remedial work (rehash the past) to recover what was lost in the conflict. Creating procovery alternate solutions is based on future desired outcomes. In recovery, there needs to be an explanation of the past so blame can be assigned. In procovery, the group can practice what I like to call "blameless resolution." Because it is future focused, positive assumptions are made about the very things that have caused the conflict. The following example shows how to find a procovery solution.

Laura is aggravated because Rick is the last one out of the office at night, and she believes he forgets to adjust the air conditioner before he leaves. Therefore, she comes in early and has to "freeze" for two hours because of his inconsideration. Rick thinks the cleaning crew may also be to blame.
Procovery Solution: *We will purchase a programmable thermostat! Let's meet in 2 weeks to see if the solution is working.*

Entering the boxing ring. One summer, I took boxing lessons. We trained three days and sparred two days each week. At first, I didn't think I was that good, but the trainer at the gym just kept encouraging me. Each day, he would pump me up like I was going to be the next heavy weight champion. We invested in all the equipment to keep me safe, but my Dad finally convinced me that the only reason they wanted me in the program was so the "real" boxers had a real person to hit instead of a punching bag. After several busted lips, numerous black-eyes, and a flattened nose that summer, I realized my Dad was a lot smarter than I had given him credit for. However, the thing I remember best from boxing is which corner I was supposed to go to when the bell rang at the end of a round. Even though 90 seconds in the ring is not that long, I couldn't wait for that bell to ring. I was safe there.

Similarly to the boxing ring, when conflict occurs in our life, we need to know what corner to head towards. The chart that follows explains several important dynamics to be mindful of as you are preparing for conflict resolution. In conflict, we want to show BOTH high value for the relationship AND address the needs we have personally. This is especially true if the conflict includes personal attacks.

Maintaining Healthy Relationships

YIELD   High Value in Relationship **HVR**   RESOLVE

Low **L**
Personal **P**
Needs **N**
Met **M**

H High
P Personal
N Needs
M Met

WITHDRAW   **LVR** Low Value in Relationship   WIN

WIN

I MUST WIN: Individuals who go to the corner of **LVR + HPNM** do not value the relationship, and their own ego needs drive their need to "win" in the conflict regardless of the cost to others. Controlling is essential to this self-serving individual who believes the organization exists to serve him. They make life difficult for others until they get their way. This profile fits the immature leader, the narcissistic boss, or the domineering spouse.

YIELD

I YIELD TO YOU: When a person retreats quickly to the corner of **HVR+LPNM**, they highly value the relationship and will relinquish their own needs and desires to maintain the relationship. A person with this profile is likely to feel insecure in their relationships or in their job. They may be enamored with the strong leader type or simply be a highly compliant person even though this corner leaves them feeling unfulfilled in the long term.

WITHDRAW

I QUIT: When the conflict reaches a certain point, the **LVR+LPNM** folks will withdraw and head for the door. This type of person will more easily abandon the relationship and their responsibilities because they find little satisfaction in them and do not value them. They often have a lack of passion for the mission and organization. They are in the classic lose-lose situation. They may sit stewing in silence, or they may slam the door on their way out. In either scenario, they have checked out.

RESOLVE

I RESOLVE: When **HVR+HPNM** intersect, you have the best case scenario. When high personal needs are being met and the value of the relationship increases, the very process of resolving conflict makes you a better person, and your team or family reaps the benefits.

Win-win happens best when this corner is chosen in advance. Predetermine that this is the corner where the greatest gains happen. Understand it requires compromise, openness, and integrity to get there. Teams that adopt this "RESOLVE corner" as their preferred choice BEFORE conflict erupts tend to make the greatest gains. High EQ enables this person to thrive in most organizations.

STAGE 2: SOLVE THE RIGHT PROBLEM

Once the preparations for conflict resolution are in place, the next stage is to understand the situation correctly and solve the right problem. It is baffling at times why otherwise well-intentioned, hard-working people can't seem to resolve conflict in their midst.

My role as a consultant at The Center gets me a seat at the table in many organizations that have become totally engulfed in conflict. I listen, I ask a few questions, and then I listen some more. Before long, the problem is so obvious to me that I can't believe they have so much time, effort, resources, and heartache wrapped up in this issue. I am not implying that the answer is always easy, but the solution is usually apparent.

I use the following chart to help groups answer the right question and therefore solve the right problem. This step alone can go a long way to resolve the conflict as it helps the team see the facts more objectively and with less emotion.

Solve the Right Problem

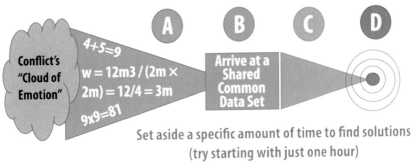

Set aside a specific amount of time to find solutions
(try starting with just one hour)

A Write down only <u>factual data</u>. No perceptions, opinions, or solutions can be offered yet. Spend 50% of your time collecting all the facts in Step A.

B Agree upon a shared set of <u>facts</u>. Spend no more than 10% of your time here.

C Narrow down the <u>interpretation</u> of the facts. What do the facts mean? What has become clear from the facts? Spend no more than 20% of your time here.

D Find <u>solutions</u> using your shared intelligence. If you spend more than 20% of your time here, you did not allot enough time in the other segments.

What I like about this process is that it creates opportunity for voice in the system without having a free-for-all. Each time segment allows input that is germane rather than providing a platform for circular reasoning, joining the bandwagon of the chronically discontent, or simply spewing toxic accusations to keep the organization in a state of chaos.

Important Note:

Knowing when to let go and give up is not always easily discerned, but sometimes, it is the right thing to do. For a variety of reasons, some conflicts end in separation, and that is OKAY. When you have made serious attempts to reconcile but have failed repeatedly, or the differences are so deep that no middle ground is acceptable, it is best to release yourself and others from further obligation. This may mean someone is transferred to a different department or asked to leave the organization. In certain cases, separation can be the healthiest resolution. In the Bible, separation was necessary to accomplish what God had intended. I can think of over 20 of these illustrations with little effort. There are enough examples throughout history to convince me that a valid strategy is to agree to disagree and part company. One classic dispute in the scriptures happens between Paul and Barnabas. These two close buds were committed followers of Jesus, but they disagreed about how to use another person in their group. The best scenario was to divide, and God blessed them both!

STAGE 3: CODIFY THE AGREEMENT

I find it is important for two reasons to have a written record of agreements made. First, conflict often behaves like a forest fire. Just when you think you have it under control, it flares up again. As time passes, a root of bitterness can still be growing just under the surface, waiting for an opportunity to trip up the peace that was agreed upon. Second, commitments without measurements become meaningless. Most often tangible agreements need to have tangible action plans to turn them into realities. It is essential to have clarity rather than ambiguity about what is expected now and in the future. Sadly, these expectations are often best articulated in separation agreements rather than peace treaties. It's one thing to shake hands and smile at each other; it's an entirely other thing to begin working together collaboratively. Consider using something like the following chart to capture the commitments.

WE HAVE AN AGREEMENT				
Agreement Statement				
What will be better in the future?				
What are the metrics of success?				
What have I agreed to NOT do?	Person 1	Person 2	Person 3	Person 4
Early indicators that the agreement may be failing				
Dates for check-ups				

STAGE 4: CELEBRATE

Forgive me if this stage sounds over simplified. The truth is we get exactly what we honor. One of the best ways to encourage strong relationships and organizational health is to celebrate the victories. When a conflict resolution process works well, celebrate it. What leaders recognize and champion is what others will emulate. A wise leader will let others have time and space to try and resolve their differences before stepping in, and when they succeed, the leader will take time to celebrate with them and acknowledge the contributions everyone made toward reaching a good solution. This can build team cohesion and confidence in their problem solving skills and can help avert further conflict. ■

QUICK REFERENCE QUESTIONS FOR WHEN CONFLICT OCCURS

1. What/who do I believe is the primary source of the conflict?
2. Is this a disagreement or is divisiveness present?
3. What has actually been lost in the conflict so far?
4. Am I personally a part of the conflict?
5. Is the conflict involving a dispute between individuals or a group?
6. Is the conflict involving staff members or programs of this organization?
7. Does this conflict put the organization at risk?
8. Who else should be informed about this conflict?
9. What should be my role, if any, at this time?
10. Is there a conflict of interest present by anyone representing the organization?
11. Do I have any legal responsibilities as a result of this conflict?
12. Is anyone in danger?
13. Are there well-established principles or policies that are being overtly violated?
14. Is the conflict simple or complex in nature?
15. Should outside expert help be sought, and if so, what kind of help?
16. Is there a long-term pattern of conflict?
17. What are the next three to five steps that should be taken?

TAKING THE NEXT STEPS

Identify three areas where you can improve your skills in conflict resolution.

1.

2.

3.

I AM NOT A PRODUCT OF MY CIRCUMSTANCES. I AM A PRODUCT OF MY DECISIONS.

STEPHEN COVEY

CHAPTER SEVEN

DELEGATE OR DROWN

BY JAY R. DESKO, Ph.D.

"

The surest way for an executive to kill himself is to refuse to learn how, and when, and to whom to delegate work.
– J.C. Penny

Henry was the CEO of a medium-sized non-profit organization with over 50 employees. The organization was effective in many ways because of Henry's influence. He had a great reputation in the industry, he had a team with a number of good employees, and there was money in the bank. But… he was drowning. The work hours were far too many, emails and texts overwhelming, problems to solve never ending, and projects to complete ever growing. Happiness was a distant memory. Many days Henry wanted to quit, and he was the CEO! You can imagine how much more stressful this work situation would feel to an average employee who doesn't have much authority or control over his or her work.

One fascinating aspect about "drowning" in life is that it is often an element essential to life, just like water, that is killing you! Water is a good thing, but an unmanaged excessive amount of it can literally bury you. The same is true for the things that were overwhelming Henry. They were all good and many were important. But if he doesn't choose a different way, he will drown. Henry is not alone. Even in ancient history, we have a powerful example through the well-known story of Moses of the challenges a leader can have with delegation. As you look at this story in the following section, doesn't it have a lot in common with Henry? Pay special attention to the colored statements that reflect the problem (*RED*) and the solution (*GREEN*) defined by Moses' father-in-law Jethro.

¹³ The next day Moses took his seat to serve as judge for the people, and they stood around him from morning till evening. ¹⁴ When his father-in-law saw all that Moses was doing for the people, he said, "What is this you are doing for the people? Why do you alone sit as judge, while all these people stand around you from morning till evening?"

¹⁵ Moses answered him, "Because the people come to me to seek God's will. ¹⁶ Whenever they have a dispute, it is brought to me, and I decide between the parties and inform them of God's decrees and instructions."

¹⁷ Moses' father-in-law replied, "What you are doing is not good. ¹⁸ You and these people who come to you will only wear yourselves out. The work is too heavy for you; you cannot handle it alone. ¹⁹ Listen now to me and I will give you some

*advice, and may God be with you. You must be the people's
representative before God and bring their disputes to him. ²⁰
Teach them his decrees and instructions, and show them
the way they are to live and how they are to behave. ²¹ But
select capable men from all the people—men who fear God,
trustworthy men who hate dishonest gain—and appoint them as
officials over thousands, hundreds, fifties and tens. ²² Have them
serve as judges for the people at all times, but have them bring
every difficult case to you; the simple cases they can decide
themselves. That will make your load lighter, because they will
share it with you. ²³ If you do this and God so commands, you
will be able to stand the strain, and all these people will go
home satisfied."*

*²⁴ Moses listened to his father-in-law and did everything he said.
²⁵ He chose capable men from all Israel and made them leaders
of the people, officials over thousands, hundreds, fifties and tens.
²⁶ They served as judges for the people at all times. The difficult
cases they brought to Moses, but the simple ones they decided
themselves. –Exodus 18*

If you ever feel like Henry (or Moses!), this chapter will be
helpful to you since your lifeline is the same as Henry's –
delegation. Delegation is entrusting a task or responsibility to
someone else who is equipped to do it.

WARNING SIGNS FOR LEADERS

Over the past 25 years of serving as a leader and a consultant,
I have seen a number of warning signs that pointed to staff
members, business owners, church pastors, and leaders
(including myself) not delegating. The following chart
describes what a leader and his or her team may experience as
a result of the leader failing to delegate.

The Leader may experience…	The Organization and Team may experience…
• Loss of passion for what he or she is doing • Working far too many hours • Inadequate time spent on vision and organizational priorities • Few new ideas or creative initiatives • Leading with "NO" more than "YES" • Declining physical or emotional health • Having trouble sleeping • Becoming emotional more easily than usual • Not meeting deadlines	• Feeling micro-managed • Having excessive meetings with supervisors • Feeling under-challenged or limited in opportunity • Important projects or tasks not being completed in a timely manner • Looking for new employment opportunities • Having to seek approval before taking action • Absence of creativity and new initiative

If some of these statements describe you, perhaps it's time to try a different approach to life and work. Start delegating! However, before we look at how to effectively delegate, let's look briefly at why we often do not.

WHY LEADERS DON'T DELEGATE

1. We don't count the actual cost of not delegating.

Ellen was a successful director of a small business with an annual budget of six million dollars, over 28 employees, and a salary and benefits package valued at over $150,000. During a coaching session, we discussed the pressure she felt and the sense of drowning she experienced as a result of so many responsibilities. I asked her to list some of the tasks she had worked on over the past month. The list was very long! Next, I asked her to identify which of these tasks only she could do. There were a number of items on this second list that I questioned. Then, I asked her this painful question: "You make about $72 per hour. Would you hire and pay an employee $72 per hour to do these same tasks?" That hurt because she realized she would never pay someone that much money to do what she was doing! This example demonstrates the point that a failure to wisely manage delegation can ultimately result in poor stewardship of your resources and a significant loss of money when extrapolated over the whole company.

2. We are concerned about the quality of the task.
Let's face it, we often just don't believe others will do the job as well as us. If we let them try and they don't perform well, how will that make us look? In some ways, there is a little narcissist residing in all of us, isn't there? While it may be true that some gifted leaders can have a magic touch in how they do certain tasks, this does not mean the task cannot or should not be delegated to others.

3. We do not have the time it takes to explain the task.
Sometimes, it is far quicker to just do something yourself, right? After all, it takes time to clearly explain what we want or to train someone to do it. However, doing it ourselves is only a short-term solution for us; it is only looking at what is urgent rather than what is important for the long term.

4. We are being shaped by the fears that lurk within us.
Fear of losing influence and authority.
Fear of giving up control.
Fear of not being needed.
Fear that someone may do a better job than us.

5. We were burned by trying to delegate in the past.
Sometimes we have delegated only to be embarrassed by the task not being completed to the quality we expected or

even at all. This can cause us to be slow to delegate again even though such a response will hold us back and contribute to the feeling of drowning.

6. We like doing the task ourselves.
Sometimes, we don't delegate for a very simple reason, we like the task! For example, even though another employee can put together the graphics for our PowerPoint presentation, we may actually like doing it ourselves because we like the creative element involved or we want it to look a certain way.

7. We have a high need for affirmation and recognition.
While few will acknowledge it, and some may not even be aware of it, we as leaders/employees like to be affirmed. Often, this recognition comes from doing something that we are good at and that others appreciate. The more they tell us how much they appreciate what we are doing, the harder it is to delegate it!

The previous seven statements are reasons why we don't want to delegate, not why we shouldn't! If you want to stop sinking and start swimming, start delegating now!

10 STEPS TO DELEGATION
1. Hire people who are trustworthy and train them to the point that you have confidence in them. If you ever lack confidence in a staff member to whom you should be delegating, ask yourself, why? Did you hire the right person? Did you provide them training and opportunities to develop the knowledge and skills? Did you give them a chance to prove themselves? Did you give them coaching if they were failing?

2. Identify five tasks or projects you should not be doing but are important enough to be done. This is hard for those of us who have become so accustomed to doing certain tasks that we no longer even think about it. However, once you get through identifying the first five tasks, you will likely have more that easily come to mind. Remember, delegation is not only about which tasks to give away, it is also about which ones to keep! Answering the following questions may help you decide which tasks to keep.

- What do you do best?
- What do you do that others cannot?
- What few things must be done exclusively by you?

Remember, not everything should be delegated and delegation is NOT a way to give you more time to play, loaf, or be lazy! It should give you more time to add value to your organization's vision and your personal health and effectiveness.

3. Identify the best people you have to do each of the designated projects or tasks. If you feel you have no one, it is a sign that you have not succeeded at Step 1! Go back to Step 1 and accomplish it!

4. Provide your employee with clear explanations, expectations, and authority regarding the project or task. What do you want? When do you want it? What parameters or boundaries must they follow? Delegation often fails because the expectations were not clear on the front end. Now, let go, and let them lead! Ask them if they are confident in being successful with the task, and if not, what it will take to become confident.

5. Provide them with regular accountability and feedback. This type of regular monitoring is done by communicating your expectations for project updates and completion dates.

No deadline often means no completion! Also, give feedback on how they are doing and agree to which communication methods you prefer for staying informed. These can include:

- E-mail
- Written updates
- Shared computer files like DropBox and Google Docs
- Regularly scheduled meetings
- Informal meetings

6. Do not allow the task to be given back to you! Sometimes people like to practice "reverse delegation." Reverse delegation is when you ultimately end up with the task back in your bin. Do not allow that to happen. Your employee needs to walk away with the project, and the project needs to remain with them, not you. Remember, only jump back in when absolutely necessary.

7. Trust them to be successful. Provide encouragement and support to let them know that you are confident in them. Sometimes we can unintentionally send a message of doubt that causes people to live up to our lack of trust by losing confidence in themselves and failing. In other words, don't interfere without a very good reason.

8. Don't expect the task to be done exactly the same way you would do it. This is not realistic and does not leave room for the task to be done in perhaps an even better way. However, it is realistic to expect that it be done to a reasonable standard and that standard should have been clearly defined in Step 4.

9. If you feel they are not succeeding, test your assumptions. Meet with them for an update. Determine if you communicated clear expectations and provided them with the resources to do it successfully. Also determine if your expectations regarding the timing, deliverables, and methods are realistic. Do not take the task back, but rather coach them to do it again and to succeed.

10. Celebrate success with them by giving both private and public recognition. Such acknowledgment will build their confidence for future projects. People pay attention to what leaders recognize and celebrate.

Moses had to humble himself and give others the opportunity to lead. He found "capable people" and entrusted them with responsibilities that they were equipped for but still had them bring the "difficult cases" to him. By delegating to your team, you are showing them that you believe in their abilities. But now that you are passing projects on to them, this doesn't mean that you are useless. There will still always be "difficult cases" which will require your expertise. Delegating will free your mind and give you time to focus on the really important matters and will also give your team the freedom they need to grow. Delegation sure beats drowning! ■

NEXT STEPS FOR DELEGATION

If you had to give yourself a grade, how effective are you at delegating?

☐ A   ☐ B   ☐ C   ☐ D   ☐ F

Why do you deserve this grade?

Below are the reasons we often don't delegate. Which fit you?
☐ You don't count the actual cost of not delegating.
☐ You are concerned about the quality of the task.
☐ You do not have the time it takes to explain the task.
☐ You are being shaped by the fears that lurk within you.
☐ You were burned by trying to delegate in the past.
☐ You like doing the task yourself.
☐ You have a high need for affirmation and recognition.

What have you delegated over the past month?
1)

2)

3)

If you had extra time, what tasks or ideas could add value to your organization and life?

Identify 5 things you could delegate, to whom, and why.

Task to delegate	Who will handle it	Why you are delegating it	Date to be delegated
1			
2			
3			
4			
5			

Who will keep you accountable in delegating?

We hope the chapters in this book have helped you become healthier and more effective in your leadership. Don't hesitate to contact us on your way to becoming a more FIT leader!

AVAILABLE SERVICES

ORGANIZATIONAL ASSESSMENT AND PLANNING

Our experienced guidance can help you discern the present state of your organization and plan for a compelling future. Our custom-designed surveys, confidential interviews, and facilitated discussions will provide you with objectivity and foresight to wisely advance your vision in an effective and healthy way. The Center team will work to ensure a healthy process, accurate information, an external perspective, and a clear plan forward.

LEADERSHIP ASSESSMENT AND COACHING

Most organizations lack an effective method for providing their leaders with feedback and coaching. Our Leader 360 and other resources are proven tools which help leaders learn and grow. Whether you are considering internal succession planning, assisting a good leader in becoming even better, or are uncertain how to help a staff member who is not succeeding, these services have proved to be an exceptional investment for hundreds of leaders.

STAFFING SERVICES

When a leadership team needs to make a staffing decision, The Center consultants are trained to help. Our staffing services include networking on behalf of your organization; assisting in the assessment, screening, and interviewing process for best-fit candidates; and onboarding the new team member(s). The Center will help you navigate your staffing needs with wisdom and care.

CUSTOM DESIGNED TRAINING

The Center team offers expert, custom-designed training for less than the cost of traditional graduate courses or professional training seminars. Custom-designed, professional training is faster, personalized, and extremely relevant to your environment. Some of our specialized training modules include Organizational Leadership; Preparing for and Leading Change; Conflict Resolution; Board Development; and Emotional/Relational Skills.

MINISTRY CRISIS SUPPORT

Our Crisis Support Service is especially designed for Christian ministries. More severe examples of a crisis include a leader involved in sexual immorality, insubordination, or financial mismanagement. More common examples are a pastor or director being asked to step down or conflict that is crippling the entire organization. Most organizations are uncertain how to lead with wisdom and integrity during such stressful times. The Center's consultants can help guide your ministry back to health.

FINANCIAL FEASIBILITY SERVICES

Every vision, plan, and priority of a non-profit organization requires finances to support it. Some leaders move forward without having an accurate understanding of whether the vision is clear and compelling and if there is support for the vision. Our experienced consultants can help you determine your level of readiness for moving forward with major initiatives, resulting in a more unified and effective launch of your vision and priorities.

ASSESSMENT TOOLS

Leader 360° Process

The Leader 360 Process includes gathering anonymous perspectives of how your leadership is viewed by you, your supervisor(s), your peers, and those who report to you. Such feedback is one of the most accurate ways to identify strengths, bad behaviors, and possible blind spots.

Work Style Profile

The Work Style Profile is a customized yet affordable assessment created by Industrial and Organizational psychologists. It focuses on traditional personality traits as well as real life behavioral characteristics that are important to most positions of leadership and management.

Pre-Hire 360°

The Pre-Hire 360 is designed to assist you in acquiring feedback on a candidate from three categories: personal, professional, and self. If integrated into the hiring process for your organization, the Pre-Hire 360 Report will provide you with insight into your critical hiring decisions.

Annual Review Process

Our easy and accurate web-based process collects and computes feedback between the employee and his or her manager to encourage meaningful feedback. This process promotes a fair and open discussion about how to maximize the strengths of each team member.

The Birkman Method®

The Birkman Method® combines motivational, behavioral, and interest evaluation into one single assessment which can be used to facilitate team building, executive coaching, leadership development, career counseling, and interpersonal conflict resolution.

Church Health Assessment

The Church Health Assessment includes our custom-designed surveys, confidential interviews, and facilitated discussions in order to provide you with objectivity and foresight to wisely advance your vision in an effective and healthy way.

Technical Testing

Total Testing provides interactive, ready to use, skills testing to measure a candidate's technical skill level in areas such as Microsoft Office, administration, accounting and finance, customer service, human resources, and more. These tests help you determine if a candidate has basic, intermediate, or advanced skills.

FEES

The Center is a non-profit organization. Our fees are determined by the services you request and your ability to pay. Don't let fees prevent you from contacting us. We will do all we can to find a workable solution for you.

CONTACT US

To learn more about how our team can assist you, please contact us at **215-723-2325** or visit our website, **www.centerconsulting.org**.

ENDORSEMENTS

"Having a place to brainstorm and process through things has helped me to grow. I am personally appreciative of The Center's work. It has helped us to be a better organization and helped me to be a better leader." – Center Client

"The team at The Center takes what I would call a 'personal investment' approach to their work. They don't feel like consultants - they feel like partners who really care about helping you achieve effectiveness in the pursuit of your goals and mission. They are trusted advisors who give you an assurance that they are 'in your corner rooting for you.' They shoot straight with you and your team - whether encouraging the positive or identifying concerns. Their advice is practical and applicable immediately. God has blessed them with great wisdom and they humbly want to share it with others." – Center Client

ABOUT THE AUTHORS

Jay Desko is the Executive Director of The Center and serves on the Senior Leadership Team at Calvary Church in Souderton, Pennsylvania. Jay brings experience in the areas of ministry assessment, leadership coaching, decision-making, and strategic questioning. Jay's degrees include a B.S. in Bible, an M.Ed. in Instructional Systems Design, and a Ph.D. in Organizational Behavior and Leadership. If you would like to contact Jay, he can be reached at jdesko@centerconsulting.org.

David Marks has over 25 years of church ministry experience including 23 years as a senior pastor. His consulting experience includes ministry assessment, leadership coaching, and strategic planning. Dave's degrees include a B.S. in Bible, an M.S. in Organizational Leadership, and a D.Min. in Leadership. If you would like to contact Dave, he can be reached at dmarks@centerconsulting.org.